'Geoff Grist is equal parts accomplished real estate agent and author. As a real estate agent, he's seen every type of property in his neighbourhood bought and sold – sometimes several times over. He knows what works. We are all just lucky that his skills as a bestselling author make it easy for us to learn from his extensive knowledge and experience!'

—**Samantha McLean**, Co-Founder and Managing Editor of Elite Agent and host of the *Elevate* podcast

'*Flip for Cash* is the must-have guide for any property investors wanting to buy, renovate and maximise their selling price. Great tips, strategies and practical advice for people wanting to build their wealth through real estate.'

—**Robert Skeen**, Director of Oasis Skeen Buyers Agents

# GEOFF GRIST

# FLIP
## FOR
# C⌂SH

**Maximise your profit when you
renovate the right apartment**

# ACKNOWLEDGEMENTS

I'd like to thank everyone who's helped me to bring *Flip for Cash* into being, particularly my wife Belinda for her encouragement and support. My thanks also go to my friends and colleagues in the wonderful world of real estate for telling me their two cents worth, and thank you to my publisher, Lesley Williams, and managing editor, Vanessa Smith, at Major Street, who are the best team in the business for their endless advice and enthusiasm.

*Old ideas can sometimes use new buildings.*
*New ideas must use old buildings.*

—Jane Jacobs

First published in 2020 by Major Street Publishing Pty Ltd
PO Box 106, Highett, Vic. 3190
E: info@majorstreet.com.au
W: majorstreet.com.au
M: +61 421 707 983

**Quantity sales.** Special discounts are available on quantity purchases by corporations, associations and others. For details, contact Lesley Williams using the details above.

**Individual sales.** Major Street publications are available through most bookstores. They can also be ordered directly from Major Street's online bookstore at www.majorstreet.com.au.

**Orders for university textbook/course adoption use.** For orders of this nature, please contact Lesley Williams using the details above.

The moral rights of the author have been asserted.

 A catalogue record for this book is available from
NATIONAL the National Library of Australia
LIBRARY
OF AUSTRALIA

ISBN: 978-0-6486626-4-8

Cover and internal design by Production Works
Printed in Australia by Ovato, an Accredited ISO AS/NZS 14001:2004
Environmental Management System Printer.

10 9 8 7 6 5 4 3 2 1

**Disclaimer:** The material in this publication is in the nature of general comment only, and neither purports nor intends to be advice. Readers should not act on the basis of any matter in this publication without considering (and if appropriate taking) professional advice with due regard to their own particular circumstances. The author and publisher expressly disclaim all and any liability to any person, whether a purchaser of this publication or not, in respect of anything and the consequences of anything done or omitted to be done by any such person in reliance, whether whole or partial, upon the whole or any part of the contents of this publication.

# CONTENTS

## PART III: RENOVATING TO SELL

# WHY PROPERTY?

It would be fair to say that I love property.

I am a Sydney real estate agent who has worked in the suburbs of Mosman, Cremorne and Neutral Bay, for more than 15 years now, and I not only help my clients buy and sell, I do it myself:

- I have purchased older-style units and updated them and resold them.

- I have purchased off the plan apartments and newly finished apartments and held them for several years and then resold them.

- I have bought a block of land and planned to build on it and then resold it, without building.

- I have bought an older-style timber house and extensively renovated it and sold it.

- I have bought and sold five other principal places of residence and have just completed a major renovation of our home of 15 years, which we have now sold for a handsome profit.

I've enjoyed a great deal of upside but also some downside – as I've learned, you can't always get it right.

The point of property investing, ultimately, is to achieve financial security, with a passive income which allows you a level of freedom and flexibility to live your life on your own terms. But why property?

The sharemarket is another popular wealth-creation vehicle and building and owning a business is also an option, rather than working for wages all your life. All three have pros and cons. I have been self-employed for most of my life, and I still am. I also have a share portfolio and have watched my shares go up and go down over time. However, I am also a property person. I love property, so for me it's an obvious choice. Your choice will be up to you.

Most Australians dream of owning property, and despite high prices and housing affordability issues it's still an achievable dream for many, if gone about the right way. Importantly, everyone needs somewhere to live, whether it's living with parents, renting or owning. The great thing about property is that it's a tangible asset and offers more scope to add value through renovations and improvements, compared to owning shares. I am an advocate of developing an investment property portfolio with at least two investment properties in two different capital cities, and preferably a portfolio of three properties in three cities.

Property ownership can help you on your journey to financial independence. Buying, holding and selling property can create opportunities and generate wealth for you. Many of the world's richest people have created their wealth through property ownership and development!

In this book I'll explain what flipping is, how to assess whether it's right for you, how to choose the right property to flip and how to renovate for maximum profit.

Happy reading!

*Geoff Grist*

# PART I:
# ALL ABOUT FLIPPING

# FLIPPING APARTMENTS

When we talk about 'flipping', what do we mean? My definition is buying a property and adding value to make it more attractive to a broader market, then selling it for a profit. Buy, renovate and sell in a short time. Flip it for cash!

For years, there have been TV shows about competitive renovations, and you must have said to yourself at some stage, 'I could do that'. Despite the ups and downs, the tears and the heartaches, the contestants always seem to come out in front: better for the experience financially and spiritually.

*The Block*, for example, has been running for more than 15 seasons now, pitching four couples of mixed work and life experience against each other to renovate the worst apartments or houses imaginable over a 12-week period. Anyone who knows anything about renovating knows that 12 weeks would be a real push; however, with the magic of television, they manage it.

Australians have also binge-watched *House Rules* for at least seven seasons, following as six state-based couples renovate each other's homes over the course of a week. With a real estate company sponsor on board, this show even gives us a before and after 'valuation' to astound us with how much 'value' the participants have added with their makeovers.

Is it even possible to renovate that quickly and add that much value to a property?

Let's do a reality TV check for a moment. These shows are designed to a format, to generate ratings. The potential profit that contestants might make after renovating a property is part of the lure to get us to watch every week. It certainly works – we love it, and the ratings are huge for these types of shows because the creators have developed the right formula.

For the record, I'm a fan – but the reason you are reading this book is to find out whether you can do it too. Well, I don't recommend attempting a 12-week turnaround on a renovation, and the 'value added' you see on the TV shows may not be typical. However, my years of experience tell me that if you do it right, then – yes, it's absolutely possible to make money flipping property.

## WHAT ABOUT BUYING AND HOLDING?

Now, let's address the elephant in the room. Most of the professional real estate advice you will hear is that flipping doesn't work. The sage advice is to buy and hold property for the long term and it will go up in value and you will make money over time. The experts say that buying a run-down house and renovating it for short-term gain is hit-and-miss at best.

For the most part I agree. If you bought a property in 1970, it would be worth more today. Even if you bought a property in 2000, it would be worth more today. However, what if you bought it at the peak of the market in 2003 and sold it during the global financial crisis in 2009? Then, even though you held the property for six years, you may only have been lucky enough to break even or you may have even lost money. The property market prices cycle up and they cycle down over years, like a roller coaster, so if you buy and sell at the wrong time, you may not make money.

My approach to flipping is different, however. I am not suggesting we flip houses. I am talking about buying units in the right location with the right bones for renovation – looking for the right home units to renovate, upgrade and sell. Then the choice is yours: you can keep the apartment and move in, you can keep the apartment as an investment property and lease it out or you can flip the apartment for cash.

## WHY APARTMENTS?

Any type of property can be flipped – houses, apartments, commercial and even industrial property – but when you think of flipping, houses may come to mind first, as they've been the most popular and talked-about option in the past. Where I live and sell real estate, we have a broad mix of houses and apartments dating from the 1900s through to present day; as in most inner-city areas, we now have more apartments than houses. Why am I focusing on the apartments? There are three reasons I believe they are a great choice for flipping if you live in an Australian city:

1. The price can be affordable.

2. They're in demand.

3. They attract a broad range of buyers.

Let's look at each of these reasons in a little more detail.

## The price is right

As prices have soared over the past ten years, houses suitable for renovation have become harder and harder to find in Australian cities. In Sydney, if you can find such a property, it's likely to cost well over a million dollars plus stamp duty. That's out of reach for most of us. Apartments are much more affordable.

## They're in demand

There is continuous demand for both houses and apartments, but there are more buyers for apartments. It's the affordability factor: apartments are one quarter to one third of the cost of a house, so many buyers on a budget are prepared to compromise their dreams of living in a house and accept that an apartment is a good alternative if they want to live in the inner city.

Some buyers, of course, simply go and buy a house further out of the city or in a rural area. There is no housing crisis in rural Australia: houses are relatively affordable in most regional areas outside of capital cities. However, people are drawn to the lights of the cities. They want to live in them and so they have to buy what they can afford, which is generally an apartment. It's a lifestyle choice.

Often, parents in my area of Sydney complain to me that houses are no longer affordable for their children. Yet, when I ask if they would expect their kids to be able to buy in London, New York, Tokyo or any other cosmopolitan, world-class city, they say, 'Of course not'. The days of affordable houses in Sydney are gone; apartments have replaced them, and the world continues to turn.

## They attract a broad range of buyers

Apartments are not just for first-home buyers. The market is broad and includes investors, second or subsequent home buyers and downsizers. First-home buyers are a broad demographic, too: they're not just twentysomethings anymore. At the time of writing, interest rates are at an historical low and many people of all ages are looking to buy instead of rent, since it may cost them about the same to pay off their own mortgage as it does to pay off someone else's via renting.

Downsizers are looking for a change after their kids have moved out on their own: a city change or a sea change or a country change. They sell the family home and invest in property for their new lifestyle needs. Often that's a city pad and a country home, purchased without a mortgage with retirement in mind. They don't need the space of a family home, and they want to spend less so they buy an apartment. They are not interested in a fixer-upper, they just want a little luxury and to be able to move straight in and enjoy their new life.

For these reasons, in this book I focus on finding the right 'home unit' rather than a house. To be clear, when I talk about 'units', I am referring collectively to residential strata title properties that exist all around Australia, which may be referred to as 'units', 'apartments', 'townhouses' or 'duplexes'. I am not referring to commercial units, retail property, retirement village dwellings, storage units or company title units, although much of what I discuss may well be relevant to these properties as well.

The terminology here is important. Back in the day, houses that were divided up into separate accommodation were simply called 'flats' and were created predominately for tenants. When people decided that living in a flat wasn't such a bad idea after all, developers started building home units. These days, all off the plan units are called 'apartments' by their marketing teams. Technically, they are 'units' on the contract of sale, but from a marketing perspective it seems they don't build 'units' or 'flats' anymore, they only build 'apartments' – which is lucky for us, because there are plenty of units out there waiting to be turned into apartments.

## HOW MANY BEDROOMS?

The lower the purchase price of a property in the right location, the lower the risk and the higher the chance to make some money. Studio units are the most affordable entry point into the property market, but one-bedroom units are the most popular entry point and are also affordable. Here are the main differences between the three most common unit types:

- **Studio units** are sometimes called bedsits and are essentially one room: a combined bedroom and living room with a kitchen on the side. They range in size from 25 m$^2$ to about 42 m$^2$.

- **One-bedroom units** have a bedroom separate from the living room and generally cost less than two-bedroom units. They range from 44 m$^2$ to about 55 m$^2$.

- **Two-bedroom units** cost more, but sometimes you may find a unit of this type that's in your budget, so let's not rule them out.

Occasionally, you will find a studio unit with the potential to change the floor plan to create a one-bedroom unit configuration. To qualify as a bedroom, the space must have an outward facing window, and ideally a window that opens. You can add a non-structural wall to a studio unit and create a separate room within the studio but, without a window, it's still a studio unit.

I recommend you look to buy a true one-bedroom unit with a window or door to the outside of the building, rather than a studio conversion. There will always be studio opportunities that are at an attractive price point, so of course the decision is yours; however, adding a wall to create a room doesn't change the physical size of the apartment, and it will still feel like a studio conversion.

My goal with this book is to help you to find and buy the right unit to renovate so that you can turn it into an apartment – because, quite simply, apartments sell for more money than units! So, is flipping apartments the right wealth-creation strategy for you? Let's explore this question.

# IS FLIPPING
# RIGHT FOR YOU?

Now that you're clear on what flipping involves, and why we're concentrating on flipping apartments rather than houses, let's get back to you.

## WILL FLIPPING WORK FOR YOU PERSONALLY?

Whether flipping property is right for you will depend on your current situation. Your relationship status, where you live now, what you do for a living and what savings you have available will all determine your suitability to flip units. Consider these factors:

- If you are single, you can make decisions unilaterally. If you have a partner or 'significant other', then your decisions need to be joint decisions, as they affect both of you. Is your partner keen or at least willing to put in the time, money and effort required to flip apartments?

- What are your skill sets? Do you work in the construction industry or have the experience to undertake this project yourself, or will you outsource this? Do you have a relative you plan to call on to manage the project for you?

- Are you mentally tough? Sometimes, things will happen that may be a lot to manage so you will need to be resilient and flexible to finish the job.

- Do you have time? What's your time worth? If you have a job, you can calculate your hourly rate and you should factor this into the project. You won't be able to pay yourself an hourly rate, but it's important to know what you may have to pay a project manager if you don't have the time yourself.

- Don't forget to account for travel time from where you live or work now to the location of the unit. Tradies start at 7 a.m. and you may have to meet a plumber onsite to open up and give directions before heading back to your own job: what's the travel time in traffic to meet your trades, and what will it mean if they are running late or need to buy materials on the way?

- If you do manage the job yourself, are you up to date with all the regulatory requirements you will be exposed to? (See appendix A for more details.)

- Will you enjoy renovating to sell, or find it a big chore? If you are not going into this thinking it's going to be fun, don't do it!

## DO YOU HAVE ENOUGH CASH?

Unlike an investment property, while you are renovating to flip, you will not have a tenant paying rent, so you will have a loan and no income from the asset to make the repayments.

Run your numbers (chapter 3 will help you with this) and seek advice about your cash flow from purchase to sale, which could be four months, six months or longer. Consider:

- Do you have enough savings to manage repayments and either work on the renovation yourself or pay others to do it for you?

- Will you need to maintain your day job to keep the money coming in?

- Are you planning on taking four weeks' holiday time from your job to save on labour and do some of the work yourself?

I recommend you create a project timeline and set realistic dates for the renovation from purchase through each major stage, so you know how much and when you will need to pay for materials and tradespeople. Allow a minimum 10 per cent contingency for things you can't plan for. (See chapter 19 for more about the scope of works and budget.)

If you don't have enough savings to pay cash for your unit and the costs of the renovation, then you will need finance provided by a bank lender (or the bank of mum and dad).

### Rule of thumb renovation budget

I suggest your renovation budget should be no more than 10 per cent of the current value of the property. So, a $500,000 property should have a maximum $50,000 renovation budget.

It's too easy to spend too much and overcapitalise. You need to keep your eye on the end prize and understand that the success of the entire project hinges on the sale price for the finished product.

If the property market is increasing during your renovation, it will help with your spend, but if it is flat or falling you may have to reconsider what updates represent value to your potential buyer. If the market falls, you may have to hold your property longer than anticipated to achieve the price you need.

All of these are factors you need to consider in your planning stage. A renovation may be a simple paint-and-carpet or it could be the full renovation where you remove walls to create an open-plan living feel. Either way, before you do anything else, talk to a mortgage broker about your financial situation so you know how much you can borrow and what it involves. A good broker will help you understand what your limits are, which will allow you to plan your next move.

Everyone is different and nothing is chiselled in stone.

## WOULD FLIPPING NEW APARTMENTS SUIT YOU BETTER?

The alternative to buying to renovate and add value is to buy a finished apartment in the first place. You can make a profit on new apartments when you sell in the short term if you know what to look for and where to buy. When looking at new properties online, consider more than just the floor plan. Have a look at the quality of finish, the colour schemes on offer, the window furnishings, the combinations of tiles, carpet and timber, the kitchen appliances and storage, and be inspired about what you can do to create a luxury haven as the professionals do.

Some investors buy 'off the plan' (that is, at the stage when there are property plans available or building is underway) with resale in mind. They then flip their off the plan properties by selling when they are complete or nearly complete. In a rising market, this strategy has merit, however in a flat or falling market you may be left 'holding the baby'.

The benefit of buying an off the plan apartment to flip is that these apartments offer a range of amenities in a brand-new building, which has definite lifestyle appeal, particularly for downsizers. Many new apartment developments are luxuriously appointed and include shared facilities such as swimming pools, gymnasiums, rooftop cinemas, private dining rooms, concierges and even wine storage and cellars. They may feature high-end retail shops on the ground floor plus signature restaurants, as destinations that draw patrons from all around the city to experience the new dining precinct and entertainment quarter that the developers are creating.

To give you a feel for the types of apartments I am referring to, have a look at the award-winning apartments built by these developers:

- Aria Property in Brisbane: www.ariaproperty.com.au

- Gurner in Melbourne: www.gurner.com.au

- Geocon in Canberra: www.geocon.com.au.

More cautious buyers may want the security that a finished property offers them. They like to be able to see and feel and walk through the finished building and experience the apartment, not just imagine it. The difference between the buyer who can see an off the plan apartment through the developers' concept plans and the buyer who needs to experience, it is often a tidy profit in a rising property market. But as we know, markets move up and down so there is risk involved.

Some investors consider buying off the plan too risky. While there are many variables to consider, the final product is a brand-new apartment in a brand-new building, which provides tax deductions for depreciation (if you're renting the property rather than living in it) and also comes with some form of builders warranty. A second-hand property has no warranty at all.

When you buy off the plan, however, you are buying into the developer's reputation. Some are good and some not so good, so do your homework. The Sydney and Melbourne newspapers have been full of stories about poor construction at time of writing. If a deal seems too good to be true, perhaps it is.

My preference is to add value to an older unit, but I have also bought apartments off the plan and also bought newly renovated property. However, if you just want to get a foot in the property market door, then buying a new apartment may be the best option for you as you will have no further expenses, willing tenants and solid depreciation.

Take some time now to think through whether flipping is the right thing for you, and ask yourself the questions listed in the box below. In the next chapter, we'll look at how to run the numbers on a flip and what to consider financially.

---

### In summary: Is renovating to flip for you?

- If you have a partner, are they on board with flipping?
- Do you have renovation-related skills? If not, are you comfortable outsourcing?
- Do you have the emotional resilience to deal with the ups and downs of renovating?
- How much time can you spare? Will you need to employ a project manager?
- Are you confident you can get up to speed on regulatory requirements?
- Do you have enough cash to fund a purchase and renovation, or can you get finance?
- Are you better suited to flip new properties at this stage rather than renovating – buying off the plan and selling post-construction?

---

# RUNNING THE NUMBERS

Property investing is all about the numbers. Let's come back to *The Block* for a moment. The purpose of the TV show is not to make money on real estate. The show is designed to entertain viewers and the more entertaining it is, the more viewers watch it, which means they can charge more for the TV ads during the show and charge 'sponsors' more to be involved. The vehicle to entertain you is a renovation show. The hook that entertains you is emotion. The TV show makes money from advertising. The TV show has a production budget to make the show. If the producers make it really entertaining and lots of people watch the show then the advertisers and sponsors will pay more than the production budget to be involved and the show is a huge success, so they can do it again next year. That's 15 years in a row so far – they have a winning formula.

That's what you need: a winning formula. Not all properties will make you money, just as not all TV shows will make money. How many TV shows can you think of that are no longer on air because viewers stopped watching them and they didn't make money? It's a risky business and so is flipping. Nothing is guaranteed; that's why it's not for everyone. While anyone can buy and hold a property for 30 years, not everyone can flip a property for cash – at all – let alone do it quickly and profitably.

When you buy property, it's important to keep your end goal in mind. There are four criteria that will affect your expected profit when you flip for cash:

1. how much value you can add to the property
2. the purchase price
3. the cost of your finance
4. your timing when you sell.

## HOW MUCH VALUE CAN YOU ADD?

My aim with this book is to help you to find and buy the right unit that suits a renovation so that you can turn it into an apartment because, quite simply, apartments sell for more money than units! My rule of thumb is that when adding value, you need to make $2 for every $1 you spend.

By selecting the right unit, you will stack the cards in your favour and be able to add value to turn a profit on resale. The more you know about a prospective building where a potential unit is available, the easier it is to decide if that unit is suitable for upgrading to make money.

While all units will benefit from upgrades, we want to choose the cream of the crop so we minimise our risk to maximise our resale prospects. Every apartment will eventually sell for the right price, but we are looking to achieve a premium price in a short time frame so we need to be a bit fussy about which unit we buy in the first place. It is possible to overcapitalise and not get your money back, so be warned.

If you walk onto a used car lot, there may be hundreds of cars to choose from: different brands, different models, different ages and different prices. If you are like me, you narrow your choice based on your lifestyle needs. If I am looking for a vehicle to help me do my renovations, I will be looking for a ute or a van, not a two-seater convertible. Even if the convertible were at a bargain price, it would be the wrong choice. I am not looking for a bargain, I am looking for the right vehicle at a price that represents good value and, most importantly, for it to do what I need it to do.

The same goes for shopping for a unit to flip. I am looking for the right unit that meets my needs and represents value. I can then leverage the unit by enhancing the look and feel to create a home that competes with new apartments for a similar price. Often, for example, older buildings are in better locations because they had the choice of sites when they were being built. So by upgrading the older unit, I am creating a product that will be in high demand for location and lifestyle.

Parts II and III of this book will go into detail about what to look for when choosing the right apartment and renovating to sell.

## HOW MUCH SHOULD YOU PAY?

If you are looking to renovate and flip, then the price you pay for a property is more important than if you plan to stay for ten years or more.

It's all about the numbers and you will want to realise a decent return on your hard work after costs to make money on your flip. Before we go any further, ask yourself if your chosen suburb/s can support a reasonable level of profit. To find out, let's look at some hypothetical numbers.

## Running the numbers: an example

Say that your budget allows you to pay up to $600,000 for a one-bedroom unit (plus $22,490 stamp duty) in Sydney. You will have an original outlay of, say, $625,000. To keep the figures simple, I am not including the cost of your money – you may have accessed savings, borrowed the sum or sold shares. Whatever you do, there are holding costs to the purchase that only you can calculate.

Let us then say you will spend $50,000 upgrading the one-bedroom unit (remember: no more than 10 per cent of your purchase price).

Your upgraded unit has cost you $675,000, plus marketing and agents' fees (real estate agent and advertising costs) on the sale of, say, $20,000. This means a final cost of $695,000 – this is your break-even figure.

What percentage of profit on the sale before tax will make the flip worthwhile for you?

- 10 per cent profit on $695,000 costs will be $69,500, thus a sale price of $764,500.

- 15 per cent profit on $695,000 costs will be $104,250, thus a sale price of $799,250.

- 20 per cent profit on $695,000 costs will be $139,000, thus a sale price of $834,000.

Are there examples of one-bedroom apartments in the same suburb that are selling for $834,000? Or are they selling for $695,000? What sort of recent sales history is there in the area?

What do these apartments look like, what do they offer, what level of quality do they provide?

What's the best-case scenario and worst-case scenario for you?

Remember, my rule of thumb on renovations is to make $2 for every $1 spent, so if I could achieve a $100,000 margin on a flip for a 15 per cent profit (based on the figures in the example above) with a turnaround time of six months, I would be happy with that. You might be different – you might want to do two flips a year, or use the profit from one flip to put a deposit down on another unit to renovate and keep it. You might even want a 20 per cent margin to make it all worthwhile. Do the numbers and see if you can make it work for you. It's your choice.

## Don't forget tax

These potential profit figures don't take into consideration your personal tax situation, which will vary for everyone. You will need to ask your accountant or financial adviser about your individual situation.

You may have purchased the unit in a company name or with multiple partners, or you may be liable for land tax if you own more than one property in the same state, which are further reasons to seek professional advice before you do anything else. (See appendix A for links to state- and territory-specific information on land tax. Note that the Northern Territory has no land tax.)

The Australian tax laws regarding property are still some of the most generous in all the world. You will generally owe no capital gains tax (CGT) on profits from a property sale if:

- the property has been your main residence (sometimes called 'principal place of residence')

- *and* you were a resident of Australia for tax purposes while you were living in the property

- *unless* you've used it to earn rent or run a business or have flipped it, depending on individual circumstances.

However, if you own two properties, say, one of which is your main residence and the other your investment property, when you sell your investment property, you will be liable for CGT. There may be an exemption in these circumstances:

- You acquired the property before CGT started on 20 September 1985.

- A rollover situation applies, wherein you reinvest in another property in a short period of time.

- Your property was compulsorily acquired.

- The property was transferred to a former spouse as the subject of a family law settlement.

When CGT is payable, it is because you have made money buying, improving and selling a residential property – it's a tax on your sale profits, not on the whole sale amount. So, for example, if you paid $300,000 for a unit and sold it for $500,000, you are only liable for CGT on the profit of $200,000, not on the whole sale amount of $500,000. Do the maths and include the CGT payment in your calculations: much of the time you may still come out in front. If the numbers show that after all your sweat and tears, it just won't be worth it, however… well, you would have to agree it's much better to find out beforehand than halfway through the project!

If you do end up making a capital loss, you can claim a CGT loss.

How much CGT you will pay or deduct will depend on your personal tax position at the time, so be sure to seek professional advice in advance to understand the implications, and to ensure that your effort in renovating to flip is a rewarding exercise and not merely break-even.

Some people will go to any lengths to avoid paying their fair share of tax, but be aware that the Australian Taxation Office has rules to prevent this. For example, if an investor owns an investment property with a remaining mortgage of $100,000, they may decide to sell it to a family member at that price, thinking they will be able to claim it as a CGT loss. However, in this case, CGT will be based on the market value of the property, not on the $100,000 that changed hands. Always ask your tax professional for advice on the sale or transfer of property.

You can find more information about CGT at the Australian Taxation Office website: www.ato.gov.au/General/Capital-gains-tax/Your-home-and-other-real-estate.

### Ownership options

When you are looking at flipping a property, there are several ways to get started to achieve the same end result. Most people buy their second property in their own name and sell it again, pay the CGT and still make a profit. Some people purchase properties through a company or trust and others may use their superannuation funds to purchase and resell property. Some set up a self-managed super fund (SMSF) to invest in residential real estate, since it became possible for SMSFs to borrow money to fund a direct property purchase. You may also be eligible under the First Home Super Saver Scheme (FHSS), introduced in April 2017, to make contributions to your super and then apply to release those contributions to buy your first home. There are restrictions on what you can and can't do with funds so, again, ask your tax adviser for advice.

A small group of investors are making property flipping their full-time business and using a mixture of strategies to acquire, renovate and on-sell investment properties with full or part equity, no equity at all and some deals that allow them to control the property with no money down. These mortgage-takeover-style strategies effectively allow a 'flipper' to take over the mortgage payments of another person who may be in mortgage distress, without paying stamp duty or mortgage set-up fees.

In effect, with the right legal documents in place, including caveats, this type of investor is controlling the property without ownership, by agreeing with the owner on a path to sale and distribution of the sale proceeds. These are time-sensitive deals with unfortunate mortgage holders who are in a distressed position. These owners can see the benefits of working with an individual investor to solve their problem as being a better option than having their loan called in by a bank, which would sell their property and retain any capital gain additional to the mortgage amount. These investors are on the lookout for mortgage-stressed property owners who may be subject to sheriff's orders, company liquidations, bankruptcies, deceased estates or divorces, and properties where the owners are simply unable to pay the mortgage and are looking for a dignified way out.

### Stamp duty

When you purchase a property, you also pay stamp duty, a state-based charge that you need to take into account when calculating whether a flip stacks up financially. Stamp duty is known by different names in different states and territories; for example, it's called 'transfer duty' in New South Wales and 'land transfer duty' in Victoria. If you purchase as a first-home buyer, you may get a stamp duty concession, but you may need to live in the property for the first six months in order to be eligible for this. Check the stamp duty rates and rules in your state with the relevant authority (these are listed in appendix A).

### Spending more or less

What happens if you spend less on the renovation – $40,000 or $30,000 instead of $50,000? What would happen to the numbers then? If you spend less, so that the apartment is of poorer quality, will you get less in return? What level of renovation investment will make the numbers work, not just for you but for the potential buyer? Don't forget that to make money, someone else has to see the value you have created and be prepared to trade you their cash for your hard work.

## Flight to quality

There is a movement among affluent apartment buyers called 'a flight to quality'. Cashed-up buyers are prepared to pay a premium price for a property that stands head and shoulders above the other properties on offer. Quality is reflected in the location, features, benefits and presentation of an apartment. The higher the quality, the design and fit-out of the apartment, the more likely buyers will be to pay a higher price. Your goal is to achieve a record price for the block or a record price for the street. This is important to keep in mind when you are doing your numbers because if you scale back on the renovation investment, you may also remove the wow factor that buyers are all looking for. Your renovation needs to stand out to attract the highest price; that means it has to offer the buyer a level of quality and lifestyle that is seldom seen. When you create desire and urgency among buyers you create competition. People want what other people want. Premium buyers want scarcity, they want something that not everyone else has, they want something special that makes them feel special and they are prepared to pay for it.

## Do your research

Your research phase is all about working out what people (the market) want and what they would be prepared to pay. Compile a spreadsheet with the buy and sell prices for similar units in the areas of interest to you. Flipping property carries some risk and it isn't easy. If it were easy, everyone would be doing it. Flipping is not for everyone, but it costs nothing to do your homework and look at the numbers to see if it is for you.

### Raising funds

If it does make sense, but you are still struggling to raise the initial investment to purchase a unit, what are your other options? Maybe you could look for a partner? Or you could talk to a friend about investing as a 50/50 partner with you. If neither of you is going to live there, maybe two heads are better than one. It's a business project, so treat it as such. Look at the upsides and the downsides and if the worst thing that happened was that the market didn't respond as well as you had hoped to your apartment, are you able to hold it and lease it for a while? Would the rent cover your loan repayments? Do your homework and weigh up the risks, then make your own decision.

## COST OF FINANCE

Even if you are not intending to hold your apartment for very long, the interest on your loan will be a considerable expense and so it pays to shop around to get the best interest rate and terms. It also helps to know how much a lender will offer you, so that you can negotiate on a potential purchase with confidence.

I meet property buyers every day who are hoping to find their ideal next home. There is a property buyer cycle that sees buyers come in to and go out of the market over time. Buyers who have all their ducks in a row are at a huge advantage to other buyers.

### Using a finance broker

The buyers with tidy ducks are working with a mortgage broker, not a single bank. A great broker is on your side and they want you to be successful and buy a property. The brokers I work with are paid by the lender when the loan is approved so there is no upfront fee for you to consult and work with this type of broker. They get paid when they organise the loan for you. The other option is to pay a loan origination fee to the broker separately. While a single bank can help you with a mortgage, you will never know if you got the best deal or not; and with interest rates constantly changing, you need a broker you can rely on.

The broker I trust compares my loan needs with 23 lenders to get me the best deal. I also refinance on my broker's advice. Different lenders will be leaders in the market at different times; consequently I have accounts and loans with six different lenders so I avoid putting all my eggs in one basket.

## Getting a loan approved

It's worth pointing out here that loan approvals are more complicated since the banking Royal Commission and the process takes time, so you really need to set up a relationship with your broker well before you find a property. Your broker will need your most recent tax returns, so be sure to have your affairs up to date. Lenders want to know about your spending habits and will analyse your credit card statements and even question some charges. I don't agree with it, but they will do it and it takes time, so don't expect to get a loan approval overnight. Your initial approval is a standing offer to lend you up to a certain amount, which can expire if you don't go ahead with a purchase within a few months.

When you do find a property you want to buy, again your broker will help you to apply for a written formal loan approval based on the property you have chosen. The lender may even request to see a signed front page of the contract of sale with the purchase amount and the property address. They may choose to do a desktop valuation to ensure you are not paying too much or they may arrange for a valuer to visit the property to submit a report to them, before they offer written approval.

Be cautious of exchanging contracts until you have written formal loan approval. Some buyers will exchange contracts with a five-day cooling-off period to wait for final approval. The cooling-off requires a non-refundable holding deposit of one quarter of 1 per cent of the purchase price. For instance, if the property price is $500,000 then the holding deposit will be $1250. On exchange, the property is deemed 'under offer' but not sold, however it is effectively 'off the market' pending finance. Often the five-day cooling-off is not sufficient time for the lender to provide formal written loan approval so I would recommend you ask for a ten-day cooling-off period from the outset. This can be extended (or shortened) if both parties agree, or the seller can refuse to extend the cooling-off and the buyer may be forced to forfeit their holding deposit and the property is released to the market again. Your broker, your agent, your conveyancer and your lender will all be working hard to avoid this, so you can see why it pays to have a good team of property professionals on your side.

## YOUR TIMING WHEN SELLING

When you buy and sell is as important in real estate as what you paid and what you sold for, and the timing will have a direct impact on your success making money. The real estate market is dynamic: it changes all the time and is affected by lots of outside forces beyond our control.

Every day in my life as a real estate agent, someone asks me, 'How's the market?' My reply is simple: 'That depends, are you buying, selling or leasing?' The truth is, the market is different for all phases of real estate.

The same goes for buyers who believe the media reports that say prices are falling. What the media rarely says is that while the overall property market may be off half of 1 per cent on prices from the same time last year (taking Sydney as an example), the market is made up of many micro markets, some of which are outperforming the overall market. The same thing happens with share prices: there is always a share that is outperforming the market despite the majority of share prices falling. That share has something special that shareholders want and it is priced accordingly.

Unlike the sharemarket, the property market is less liquid, meaning it takes longer to sell a property than to sell a share. This means that price changes take longer to happen. The housing market doesn't drop one day and recover the next day; rather, it moves in waves over weeks and months, sometimes up and sometimes down depending on supply and demand.

The property market is also subject to seasonal influences and is traditionally less active in winter than summer, so as a rule of thumb you could look at buying in May/June and selling in October/November with a six-month turnaround for any renovations. If you don't sell before Christmas, the January/February market is traditionally high-performing as buyers who missed out the previous year are committed to buying in the New Year.

We'll look further at how to decide when to sell in chapter 21, at the end of this book. Now that you have an idea of how to run the numbers on a potential flip property, let's take a quick look at the ins and outs of strata title property before we move on to Part II: Choosing the right apartment.

# A LITTLE ABOUT STRATA

If you've never owned strata title property before, it's worth spending some time going over the ins and outs so you can be really sure that flipping apartments is the right strategy for you.

As the owner of a strata unit, you own the air within the walls of your unit, while the owners corporation owns and controls the building and the land around it. On paper your ownership will be of a 'lot' within the strata plan and will extend to shared ownership and responsibility for any common property such as gardens, entrances, driveways, hallways, elevators and stairwells.

Being a part-owner of this common property, you will contribute to the running costs and maintenance of the building by paying a regular strata levy, based on your share in the strata plan (called a 'unit entitlement'). This is in addition to your local taxes and rates. A one-bedroom unit of 50 m$^2$, for example, will have a lower unit entitlement and therefore a lower quarterly levy than a larger 80 m$^2$ two-bedroom unit.

This is where houses and units differ. With a house, you are solely responsible for the repairs and maintenance of your property; with a unit, you are a part-owner and each owner contributes a regular fee (quarterly or annually) for the ongoing maintenance of the property (see chapter 9 for more details).

If you can afford a house to renovate, don't let me stop you! Freestanding Torrens title houses have very few restrictions on them compared with strata title units; however, they will cost considerably more to purchase than a unit in the same suburb.

The restrictions on units will be itemised within the strata scheme rules and by-laws and will often include rules around car parking, noise control, hanging of laundry, pet ownership and even barbecues on balconies. Our interest is in the restrictions around renovations and in what has been done before and can be done again to add value to a unit.

## THE ORIGIN OF STRATA TITLE

Originally, buildings with multiple owner-occupiers were developed as company title properties. Buyers purchased shares in a company which owned the physical building and, within the laws of the company shareholding, they were entitled to occupy a specific unit. However, as buyers were not allocated independent ownership of their lot, banks were hesitant to fund these types of homes. Thus, on 1 July 1961, the *Conveyancing (Strata Titles) Act* was established as a New South Wales Government initiative which has been replicated around Australia and many parts of the world.

The legal framework has been revised and updated several times, including the *Strata Titles Act 1973* and the *Strata Schemes Management Act 2015* and Strata Schemes Management Regulation 2016. This has been done to adapt to the changing needs of strata living while providing a vehicle for individual ownership of a scheme which also allows for shared ownership of common areas, managed by an owners corporation. As regulations became more complex and properties changed hands, owners corporations appointed strata managers to manage the day-to-day running of their buildings. There are now more than 270,000 strata schemes registered in Australia, accounting for in excess of two million individual lots. In Sydney alone, more than half of all residential sales and leases are for strata titled properties.

Each strata scheme property will share the agreed strata by-laws. As a lot owner, you are required to adhere to these by-laws, which will often include general use of the common property, safety and security, noise control, rubbish disposal, the behaviour of residents and the appearance of the building. While living within the rules of a strata scheme may appear onerous on the surface, the rules are designed to help maintain harmony within a group of people sharing close quarters and using common property at the same time. From time to time there will be disputes, but there are also recognised and defined pathways to ensure disputes are resolved with the minimum of effort.

## THE STRATA MANAGER

Strata scheme properties will almost always employ a strata manager, also called an owners corporation manager or a body corporate manager.

Some buildings where there are only two or three apartments may self-manage rather than pay an external manager. They are still required to meet the guidelines for strata management but as there are so few owners, they may decide to do the job themselves: appointing one owner as president of the owners corporation, another owner as secretary and maintaining their own records of annual general meetings (AGMs) and expenditure. Some small buildings may not have common areas and the two owners will literally look after their own maintenance as if the property were Torrens title. Others may share the costs associated with the roof and garden but look after all other maintenance themselves. The main cost to these self-managed properties may simply be the annual building insurance policy, which is paid by each party depending on their unit entitlement.

In all other cases, the members of the owners corporation appoint a strata management company that in turn allocates a strata manager to manage the property alongside the owners corporation. The owners corporation is made up of apartment owners who volunteer to work with the appointed strata manager to ensure the building complies with all regulations in accordance with the *Strata Schemes Management Act 2015*. The corporation (committee) members (also known jointly as a strata committee) may change as owners buy and sell in the building, so a reliable and stable strata manager is extremely valuable to the ongoing running of the property. From time to time, the owners committee may lose faith in their strata manager and appoint another manager or management company as they see fit.

The basic roles of the strata manager can be summed up as:

- organising and running owners corporation meetings
- financial management (current and forecast expenditure)
- keeping abreast of strata laws, regulations and building compliance
- taking responsibility for building maintenance, insurance and risk management
- resolving disputes to maximise harmony among owners.

To manage all these variables on a day-to-day basis is a full-time job for an experienced strata manager, who must also be part psychologist and mediator to minimise any conflicts between parties.

In a nutshell, the role of the strata manager is to provide services to the owners of a strata scheme, represented by the owners corporation, in relation to the running of the whole strata scheme.

> ## What is the role of a property manager?
>
> The role of a property manager, on the other hand, is to facilitate liaison between landlords (owners) and tenants of a specific lot within the strata scheme. Property managers are employed by a real estate agency office to manage an individual property for an owner. Their role is to negotiate the lease of the unit, collect the rent, manage the tenants and conduct condition inspections at the property. As you can appreciate, this is a completely different role to that of a strata manager.

To renovate a unit, we must communicate with the strata manager who, in turn, checks we are within the by-laws and refers any requests to the owners corporation (committee). So the right sort of strata manager (who is capable, efficient and knows their stuff) is very important in helping us reach our end goal.

Strata units may sound like they involve a lot of extra effort over Torrens title homes – and they can, it's true, particularly when it comes to renovation. However, bear in mind this fact: although I have been selling property for 15 years, I have never sold the perfect home.

Buyers will always say that something isn't quite right for them, but they still buy the home anyway, intending to renovate. Years later, however, more people than not will have left the property as it is – they have become used to it. Renovating is a skill: it takes time, money and design sense to get it right. The fact that so many people don't want to renovate provides a huge opportunity for those of us who will renovate – and I always have more buyers for a renovated and finished property than a property that needs fixing up. Most people are time-poor and will pay a premium for a renovated property.

Sold on the idea? Then let's find out what to buy.

# PART II:
# CHOOSING THE RIGHT APARTMENT

# YOUR TARGET BUYER

The goal of our flipping strategy is to buy a unit and add value for resale. That's the whole plan, and while it seems simple enough, there are many variables to get right to ensure we maximise our profit or make a profit at all. As flippers, we are looking for units to which we can add value that will have the greatest appeal to the most buyers. To avoid wasting our time, we need to know what type of unit we are looking for so we can shortlist those that suit us best.

I always like to start with the end in mind, so before we do anything else, we should consider who will be the likely buyer of our finished apartment. Who is our target market?

A buyer's motivation to immediately purchase an apartment needs to be very high to create the emotion of 'fear of missing out' (FOMO). As a real estate agent, if I have two motivated buyers engaged with the same property at the same time, I have the perfect storm for a premium price.

One of the problems with buyers, however, is they don't know what they want. Some buyers tell me that they won't know what they want until they see it. That means they will be looking at anything and everything within their budget, which may take months. When I ask a buyer what they want in a unit, they often say things like, 'Oh, you know, the same as everyone wants... a good location, not a busy road, a good size with an internal laundry, a balcony with a sunny aspect, and parking, either undercover or in a lock-up garage'. So, if that's what everyone wants, then that's what we need to buy to renovate for resale.

As I touched on in chapter 4, more buyers want to buy a finished apartment than a fixer-upper unit. That's easy for us, then: we want an unrenovated unit which ticks as many of the buyers' criteria as possible.

## NARROWING IT DOWN

We do need to narrow things down a bit further, however. Being more specific about the particular type of buyer you want to attract to your apartment, and honing in on their particular desires, will help you to select and renovate your unit according-ly, to achieve the best sale price.

My thoughts on this are that my finished apartment should appeal to a cashed-up demographic looking for some luxury and easy access to the city. In my mind, I am looking for an own-er-occupier rather than an investor. The apartment will appeal to both types of buyers but chances are the owner-occupier will pay more than the investor, even if the owner-occupier wants to lease out the apartment for now and move in down the track.

Property ownership is about much more than a checklist of wants or needs: it's emotional. In the same way as we fall in love with a person, we can fall in love with a place, a suburb or a home. Our ideal buyer is an emotional buyer, not a logical buyer, because emotional buyers will pay more.

My target buyer is a downsizer looking for a 'city pad', not a family home. They are cashed-up and they want a relatively luxurious place in the city, a lock-up-and-leave that they can come and go from when they catch up with friends and enjoy all the entertainment options that the big city offers. You might be thinking of targeting buyers looking for a sea change, so a unit in a popular seaside suburb might be more your thing. Or with a mountain retreat, you may be targeting buyers who want a weekend escape to the mountains or the country. One-bedroom units offer lots of options in many different places; it's up to you to decide what makes sense to you.

These are my thoughts on my target market, but yours may be different – and that's okay.

# 6

# LOCATION

Once you know your target market, you can start making a short list of suburbs of interest. You cannot change the location of your ideal apartment once you buy it, so you need to choose the most attractive suburb for your target market.

Importantly, you are not going to live in this unit. I know that many investors won't buy a unit unless it is in a suburb they would live in themselves. If your plan is to live in the unit, that's fine, but if it is to sell it for a profit then your goal is to find a location that suits your target market, not yourself.

If you have always lived in the inner west of Sydney, you may not be thinking of buying on the lower North Shore. If you have always lived on the lower North Shore, you may not be thinking of buying in the inner city. It's not about you, however, it's about finding a location in a suburb with attractive resale options that will appeal to cashed-up buyers, and the first of those is transport related. In most cases the closer the unit is to the vibrancy of the city, the higher the price and the smaller the size. Our goal is to provide a bit of luxury – and in my mind, space is luxury, so I am looking for a unit with size on its side as well. Thus, a unit with good proportions and easy access to city transport are our first two buying criteria.

## TRANSPORT HUBS

My suggestion is to make a short list of suburbs that have a stand-out public transport option for easy access to the city's CBD. For instance, in Sydney, suburbs that have a ferry service to the city are highly desirable. So are suburbs that have a metro, tram or train station providing a short trip to the city, and suburbs that have an express bus to the city. Suburbs within easy cycling distance are also popular, where you don't have to have a car to access the entertainment precincts of the city, the theatres, cinemas, restaurants, parks, art galleries, pubs and public events that draw crowds.

Properties closest to these all-important transport hubs will have more noise and traffic than those a few streets away, of course. Everything is a compromise – as I said, I have never sold the perfect property.

### Sold story

I recently sold a two-year old, one-bedroom apartment with a high-quality finish that backed onto a railway line. The noise from the trains passing was too much for me but not so for the buyer, who was used to train noise and loved the proximity to the station. What I felt was a negative, he felt was a positive. Public transport does that to some buyers, they seem to be quite forgiving about properties that are very close to transport. However, not everyone is so forgiving about planes overhead, so properties that are under a flight path will be less predictable sellers than those with clear skies above them.

That said, I should also add that over the years, when the property market is down the first properties to take a hit are those on busy roads. When the market slows, buyers become picky; any properties that offer certain challenges are marked hard by buyers and they take a lot longer to sell. When the market is hot, buyers look for busy road properties to try to get into a suburb at an entry-level price.

## OLDER STYLE IN A GOOD LOCATION

Historically, many of the first unit buildings were often built in some of the best locations simply because land was available back then. These older-style buildings would have originally been company title but many have now been converted to strata title, so they are certainly worth a look. Smaller buildings of four units may also have been originally owned by one person or one person controlled the company that owned the building. Sometimes they lived in one unit and rented the others out or, over time, they converted them to strata and sold them off one by one. It is likely that many of these types of units will be largely original, which makes them suitable for renovation and resale.

Depending on your suburb of choice, you may find unit buildings from the 1920s that were built in the Art Deco style and from the 1930s built in the P&O style. Both styles are highly sought after for their architectural design, as they simply don't build units like that anymore. They will often feature curved walls and built-in features, high decorative ceilings, timber floorboards, fireplaces, picture rails and stained-glass windows. They often only have a small balcony and rarely include car parking.

## NEIGHBOURS

Individually, neighbours come and go in the same building but the neighbours in the buildings you have on either side of you will have an impact on your quiet enjoyment of your home. If there is a hotel or pub next door, you can expect some level of disruption from patrons coming and going, drunk or otherwise. Often it's simply the long goodbye that takes its toll the most – a group of friends standing on the footpath, talking far too loudly and taking far too long to say good night.

Be mindful of shops that take deliveries very early or extra late, refrigerated trucks double parked, broken bottle collection, musicians leaving after midnight, petrol stations close by and restaurant patrons leaving late at night. You won't be able to change their behaviour so it's better to avoid it in the first place. Believe me, the neighbours never seem to move but lots of people move because of the neighbours.

Remember, we are looking to minimise our risk by avoiding buying properties that may not suit our target market. Once you do buy a property, you can't change the address so make it a priority to buy a unit at the best address you can find. I have heard it said by investors that you ensure your profits when you buy, not when you sell.

### Sold story

I sold a three-bedroom apartment for downsizers who had been there less than a year. After the sale, they told me they had made a big mistake buying strata. They just couldn't get used to all the rules and in particular one neighbour who thought he owned the building and was always telling them what to do. They said they would move further away and buy a house again as they just couldn't deal with life in a strata building.

## SEARCHING FOR PROPERTIES

The first place to find property is online, so be sure to set up email alerts for a property match on one of Australia's major property portals: www.realestate.com.au and www.domain.com. au. Keep your buying criteria broad so that you receive lots of matches; it's better to see more options and cross them off as you go than not to receive any matches. Set up an account on each website and register to buy in your key suburb, and tick the box for surrounding suburbs also. Then add property type – apartment or unit – and add the maximum price that you will spend. That's it. There is no need to put number of bedrooms or minimum price, it's better to see everything available at the start so you can see what your money will buy. As you get a better feel for the neighbourhood, you can introduce new criteria to tighten your search but, for now, research as much as possible. Part of your research for an unrenovated unit will include looking at renovated apartments for sale, to see what level of quality is on offer and at what price.

I suggest you set up a spreadsheet to track properties in your chosen suburbs. Use columns for number of bedrooms, number of bathrooms, parking, balcony, air conditioning, views and proximity to transport. Also include a column for the level of renovation, so you can compare units with finished apartments for sale and then follow these properties to see how long they take to sell and what the final sale price is. This is all good research to enable you to track your market. How many unrenovated gems come onto the market and how quickly do they sell? Are there similar renovated properties on the market? If so, what are they selling for and how long does it take to sell them? This comparative data will help you determine whether your chosen suburbs have the capacity to deliver the property you want and the upside you need to make it all worthwhile.

# 7

# SIZE AND FLOOR PLAN

Space is luxury. If you book a standard hotel room and you check in, it's not so bad... it's not big but it's only for sleeping in, right? Then the phone rings and the manager offers to upgrade you to a suite. It's in the same hotel, at the same address, but it's bigger. The size means that the space feels much more luxurious, even if it's fitted out at the same level. Given a choice, everyone wants the suite because they want the space that allows them to stretch out a bit and feel a bit spoilt. In real estate, size matters!

When you start to look at properties online, be sure to open the floor plan diagram. You need to know the size and layout of the unit and how it compares with others in the building. Not all one-bedroom units are the same size, nor two-bed or even three-bedroom units. It's worth finding out if the unit you are considering is the smallest or the largest in the building. Most real estate agents will provide a floor plan drawn up by a professional floor planner. Some floor plans will include the size of the unit, as provided by the floor planner. There may be an overall size listed that includes the apartment itself and the balcony, with a separate figure for car parking and any storage, or it could be simply one figure overall.

The floor plan may not be drawn to scale. Read the disclaimer carefully, so you are aware of what is being presented to you. The disclaimer will often say something along the lines of, 'This drawing is indicative only and all dimensions are approximate, all information contained herein is gathered from sources we believe to be reliable, however we cannot guarantee its accuracy and interested persons should rely on their own enquiries'. In other words, buyer beware.

The overall size of the unit and the floor plan both matter. If the floor plan itself is not great, it may be possible to change it but if the internal size is too small, you can't change that.

## SIZE AND FINANCING

Overall size is a very important criterion for finance lenders to determine whether they will lend funds on a unit or not. They have their own minimum size lending requirements against which they will set their LVR or Loan to Value Ratio. Lenders use the LVR to decide your risk profile when determining what percentage of the loan you are seeking to borrow for the unit. For instance, a bank may have a policy that their minimum size for a one-bed unit is 50 m$^2$. Against this, they may limit their LVR to 90 per cent including a cap on the Lenders Mortgage Insurance (LMI), which is required for all borrowers at this level. Some properties with living area size of less than 40 m$^2$ are unacceptable security for LMI or Low Deposit Premium (LDP).

Different lenders will have different lending criteria at different times, so not all lenders will lend on every unit. For example, some lenders will not fund studio units at all, they must have a separate bedroom. Some will finance down to 40 m$^2$ units if they are one-bedroom and located in high-demand capital city metropolitan locations only. Another lender will fund 40 m$^2$ units excluding balconies and car spaces, however they must be self-contained with kitchenette, bathroom and internal laundry, and they will have a maximum LVR of 80 per cent. Another will fund down to 35 m$^2$ with an LVR up to 65 per cent. Ask your loan broker to provide you with a current chart of lenders' criteria.

To know the actual size of the unit you need to view the strata plan, which is included in the contract of sale. Every contract will have a site drawing of the strata plan layout of the building with measurements and orientation in relation to the street. It will also have a schedule of lot entitlement, so you can see the allocation of units, and a drawing of each floor of the building, with individual units surveyed, showing wall shapes and overall size. This diagram is prepared by a surveyor, so it will have a scale to reference and, depending on the date the strata was registered, there may be a size conversion chart from feet, inches and square feet for working out the measurements in metres and square metres. For example, a property of 548 ft$^2$ converts to 50.9 m$^2$ and that 0.9 m$^2$ may be the difference between obtaining funding with your lender of choice or not.

It's also worth noting that the whole strata scheme lot entitlement and fees payable are calculated based on the size of the unit.

## CAN YOU ALTER THE FLOOR PLAN?

After years in this business, I have a level of comfort when I walk into a one-bedroom unit that is 50 m$^2$ or larger; it feels about right and it can even feel a little bit larger depending on the floor plan. If the floor plan is wrong, I can tell almost immediately. It's then a matter of trying to decide if the floor plan can be improved or not, depending on the layout of the rooms and the location of structural walls. While you can't change the internal size of an apartment, how that space is designed and presented will change the feel of the size of the property to buyers. Perception is everything when it comes to creating emotion.

The existing floor plan is the key to our ability to add value. Can the floor plan be altered to add value? Is there a precedent in the building that gives you hope that you may also be able to change the floor plan? Maybe a previous owner has joined two one-bedroom units together to create a larger space. Sometimes you can change a two-bed unit into two one-bed units. You will need a structural engineer to confirm if walls can be moved or not. In a strata building it's not just about you, it's about all the other owners as well, so everything needs to be done by the book.

The most common update for an older-style apartment is to open up the kitchen to the dining or living room by removing a wall or part of a wall. In this way, you create an open-plan living room which connects the kitchen to the living space to make it an all-inclusive space. Look for a floor plan that offers this opportunity and, chances are, someone else in the building may have already done the same thing.

## Sold story

I sold a two-bedroom apartment that the new owners converted to a three-bedroom apartment. The main bedroom was oversized and it had a full-length wall on the hallway with the door at one end. The new owners saw the value they wanted to add to the apartment and put it all in writing to the owners committee for approval. They then added a wall at the end of the master bedroom and a second door off the hallway into the new third bedroom. They added extensive built-in wardrobe space and a study desk, so that for their own use the third bedroom was actually a study and a walk-in robe but for future sale it was a functioning third bedroom.

Of course, even if I feel I can change the floor plan for the better, I can't do a thing without the approval of the owners corporation. That's why an active strata manager is helpful in working with the owners corporation to get things done. However, the strata manager represents the current owners and not potential buyers so it is next to impossible to have a meaningful discussion with them unless I am an owner in the building, as I am not recognised as having an interest in the building. They would likely consider me a time-waster.

That's why the strata by-laws in the contract are so important, as are the minutes of the owners corporation AGM. The real estate agent should provide an up-to-date strata report (see chapter 16) compiled by a third party from the records on hand at the strata manager's office. Reading these, you can get a good feel for the attitude of the owners in relation to things like renovations, air conditioners, windows and floor coverings. You can also see if the building is up to date with fire ordinances, window locks and other regulations and get a feel for the general harmony in the building and if there is any outstanding matter or upcoming discussion that may require a special levy from owners.

Lastly, if the unit really is of interest to you, and you are still curious as to how progressive the owners corporation may be, doorknock some neighbours in the building. Explain that you are an interested buyer and ask if they know of anyone who has renovated, moved walls, updated bathrooms or added air conditioning, to see who may have set a precedent in the building. If you can speak with that owner, you may also be able to see what they have done to add value to their apartment. If you search the building address online, a recent sale in the building may appear in the real estate archives and if it was marketed through public channels, there may be photographs and a floor plan to view, plus of course the all-important sale price and date of sale.

You are still very much in your research phase so the more you know about every potential unit, the easier it will be to short-list your favourites.

While we know what we want to buy, we may have to compromise along the way. It's important to be open-minded about which properties will allow you to add value for resale. You may find a cracker of a property that has everything you want except one crucial thing, and it may still be the right property if the location or views allow you to offer 'something really special'.

## Sold story

I sold an apartment where the architect owner added an ensuite bathroom to a bedroom to create a two-bed, two-bath apartment. The existing bathroom had a door from the hallway and was a generous size so this owner reconfigured it. He removed the bathtub, freeing up even more space, and built a wall to create an ensuite into the adjoining bedroom via a sliding door. As plumbing is built into the concrete floor and your floor is the ceiling of the unit below, you can't just go digging up the concrete floor. You can, however, use the existing floor drainage and pipe water flow to it above the floor, then box in the new pipes so they are not seen and become part of the overall design. Once you get a feel for what other people have done in the past you can start to imagine what you can do when you see a property for the first time.

# 8

# THE BUILDING

No matter what, you can't change the age of a building. Every strata scheme building has a strata plan number. Strata plans originated in July 1960 and are sequentially numbered on the date they were registered. The registration date may be the equivalent of when a building was completed and registered, unless the building was previously a company title building that was converted to strata title later. However, for the most part, the date the strata plan was registered is the date a building was completed, so that is our best guide to the age of a building.

The age and the style of a building go hand in hand. I have already mentioned Art Deco and P&O styles. Moving on from then, red bricks were prevalent in the 1960s and blonde bricks were popular in the 1970s. Dark bricks with blonde brick trim featured in the 1980s. While there are no hard and fast rules, different decades took us in different directions and that included varied room shape and size, larger balconies, large separate internal laundries, combined toilet and bathrooms instead of stand-alone toilets and separate bathrooms, and

2.4 m minimum ceiling height. Developers built to a budget and most properties looked the same. Buyers accepted mediocre as standard. There was little choice.

Older units enjoyed timber floors while later units boasted concrete floors. Kitchen benches evolved from timber and tile to yellow and green Laminex, then laminated timber to natural or man-made stone. Older units had cast-iron plumbing on the outside of the building while more recent units had concealed plumbing. Many suburbs were dominated by developers who knocked down single level homes and built rows of three-storey units only differentiated by a wrought iron name on the street facing wall. A popular design offered street level undercover parking on the ground floor with a stairway entrance to a three-storey building that did not need a lift. Elevators were expensive and added to the maintenance costs as well, so developers avoided them.

Popular building names included location-based descriptions such as Eastview, North Terrace and Westleigh, while others honoured the previous owner's name such as Ayleen, Corrine or Bethlyn. These days, luxury apartment buildings enjoy aspirational names like Infinity, Metropole or The Establishment. Modern names like these make buyers feel, 'I want to live there!'

## BIG OR SMALL BLOCK?

When I sell any strata building, one of the first questions buyers have for me is, 'How many apartments are in the building?' It's a non-negotiable: you can't change the number of properties in a building, so work out your preference. The easiest way to know how many apartments are in a building is to simply count the letterboxes.

Strata levies are a fact of life for strata ownership; the maintenance of the building will be divided among all the owners.

Buyers are mindful of ongoing costs, and the number of units and the facilities included in the building will contribute to determining the quarterly contribution of each part-owner.

Many buyers tell me they prefer a boutique building of four to twelve units because it is more 'manageable', meaning that they expect with fewer owners there will be fewer expenses and less can go wrong. The biggest expense in an apartment building is likely to be the elevator: it needs regular maintenance and over time wears out and must be replaced. All owners, even the owners who live on the ground floor, contribute to the costs of the elevator through their quarterly building contributions. The more apartments in the building that contribute, the lower the quarterly contribution for each owner for the elevator.

Small blocks that don't have lifts will have ground floor units, some with a courtyard or garden which will either be 'on title' or 'shared use'; they will also have up to three levels with stairs. Buyers will either 'do' stairs or they won't. Older buyers would rather have a building with a lift because even if they can manage the stairs now, they are thinking of when their knees might give out and they will need the lift.

Small blocks with three-storey walk-up units are popular with younger buyers who appreciate that often some type of outlook or view will be gained by climbing the stairs. They also like to be the top unit so that they don't hear anyone living above them, even if the building has concrete floors in between. They would rather make the noise for someone else to worry about than be the unit underneath that hears the noise.

You need to decide what you want. Will your future buyer be happy with stairs or will they insist on a lift? This one decision alone will halve the suitable properties available for you to buy.

## THE 75 PER CENT RULE

If you are a buyer in New South Wales, you should also be aware of the 75 per cent rule. This rule states that if you own a unit in a strata building of four units and a developer approaches the four owners to buy the building, if three of them agree to the sale (that is, 75 per cent of the owners) then the fourth owner has to sell whether they agree to sell or not.

Many smaller, older unit buildings are sitting on large blocks of land which are very attractive to developers. In Victoria, the 75 per cent rule only applies if there are no opposed votes as per section 171 of the *Owners Corporations Act 2006*. Other states will have their own variation on this rule; for instance, in Western Australia, the threshold for terminating a strata was raised from 75 per cent to 80 per cent, and small strata schemes of less than five lots still require unanimous agreement. Laws in this area are still evolving, so it is recommended you check the current legislation for your own state, particularly in relation to individuals holding out against the majority in a strata building (see appendix A for details of how to access the legislation).

The higher the number of units in the building, the less likely a developer will be able to get 75 per cent agreement to sell from owners. A ten-storey building with 60 units will require 45 owners to agree to sell, but if the building is on a 5000 m² block with gardens and possibly a swimming pool, it may still be a target for developers anyway. The other target for developers is adjoining sites. Two or three small unit blocks in a row may allow the developer to amalgamate the sites, particularly if one building has two street frontages, allowing for improved car access and parking options.

## Sold story

I sold a unit in a block of four one-bedroom units for $750,000. Six months later a developer approached all the owners and three agreed to sell. The developer then optioned the building with a $40,000 non-refundable deposit paid to each owner while he sought council permission for redevelopment. The reason for his interest was that the small block of four one-bed units, two on the ground floor and two on the first floor, occupied a site with a land size of 850 m$^2$. The developer was able to have plans approved through council to extend the existing building and add four units in a separate building on the same site. The option was taken up and the developer paid the four owners $1 million each to vacate. I was then able to help two of the four owners to purchase another unit each up to the $1 million mark, which was their new budget.

# 9

# STRATA FEES AND MAINTENANCE COSTS

The strata manager, in consultation with the owners committee, sets the strata levies to be paid by each owner at the annual general meeting (AGM). They do this by examining their past, current and forecast expenditure in relation to their financial statements and the money they already have in the bank. Based on what maintenance has been done in the past, what needs to be done now and what is forecast to be done over a ten-year period, the committee will agree on the total amount of funds required and when they need to be collected. This is then divided among the unit owners according to their strata entitlement and the committee sets the quarterly, biannual or annual fees payable by each owner to cover both capital works and administrative expenses.

## CAPITAL WORKS

There is no formula for how much money should be in a capital works (sinking) fund at any one time, as it will vary according to money raised and money spent, particularly after a major piece of maintenance like having the building painted. Funds required will be determined by the building's design, amenities, features, inclusions, history, age and condition, and upcoming high-cost maintenance items such as window and balustrade replacement.

A healthy sinking fund is useful not only for the owners but us as buyers. For example, if a building has, say, 12 units and the current balance of the sinking fund is $60,000 – which is an average of $5000 per unit – as a buyer you enjoy the benefit of this balance. You can't access the money individually but it's as if you get a $5000 credit towards your unit. On the other hand, if the sinking fund has only $10,000 in it at the time you buy, you can almost predict that fees will be increased or a special levy applied to raise the current balance over the coming year.

### Sold story

I sold a one-bedroom apartment in a building with 73 units built in 2000, which had two lifts, underground parking and an internal swimming pool. However, the building was in need of maintenance and there was not enough money in the sinking fund. Rather than introducing a special levy, the owners agreed to increase the strata contributions and this one-bedroom unit had a fee increase from $890 per quarter to $1999 per quarter. The committee effectively doubled the contributions, which would be in place until the funds had been raised to pay for the maintenance issues.

Some buildings have the benefit of external income, particularly those on a ridge with an unobstructed outlook that can lease roof space to telecoms for installing cellular telephone towers. The jury is still out on the effect of these towers on residents, however some buyers will have a problem with the towers and others won't. The income generated can be significant and it can all but fully subsidise strata fees in a building.

## ADMINISTRATION AND EXPENSES

The strata manager administers the funds in accordance with the owners corporation directives and current legislation in the relevant state or territory. Typically, a building has expenses that include insurance, utilities like gas, water and sewerage, property management by the strata group, repairs and maintenance including pest control, property taxes and administrative costs.

In New South Wales, for instance, the Strata Schemes Management Regulation 2016 requires that a minimum public liability amount of $20 million per claim is provided for. Under the New South Wales *Environmental Planning and Assessment Act 1979* and the Environmental Planning and Assessment Regulation 2000, relevant buildings require annual inspection by fire control contractors in accordance with fire safety requirements. While you might expect a building to be fully compliant for fire safety, it may be a work in progress and the building may require a special levy to raise the funds to make it compliant. Buyers are advised to make their own checks, including on the annual fire safety certification statement for the building. Make sure you're aware of the regulatory requirements in your state or territory – appendix A has some links to helpful websites.

To understand if a building is 'typical' in its class, you need to compare its benchmark figures with those of, say, three other similar buildings, which will give you a feel for what level of costs seem about right. Accessing historical operating data allows you to analyse expenses in all areas for the building you're interested in, to see if there are any red flags that indicate an ongoing problem and therefore an ongoing expense.

## STRATA REPORT

When I sell a strata property, it's important to me to understand the way the building operates so that I can pass on any information that I know to prospective buyers. To do this, I request the owner to engage a third-party strata consultant to create a strata report for the sale property. This is paid for by the owner and gives me, as the agent, a snapshot of the building in time. When a buyer has expressed interest in the property, they will request a contract of sale be forwarded to their conveyancer. Their conveyancer will ask if a strata report is available; if it is not, then they will recommend their client commissions a report. They can do this by hiring a third party to attend the strata manager's office and 'look at the books' then compile a report for their client, for a fee. This may take several days depending on the availability of parties involved.

To save time and save buyers money, on request we make our strata report available at no charge as an information tool only. No opinions are expressed, only the facts are provided. These include historical expense data and financial statements. If the selling agent can supply a strata report with this information, that's a great place to start. If they can't, then you will need to commission your own report or make an appointment to attend the strata manager's office to look at the books yourself. In chapter 16, we'll cover strata reports in more detail.

## MAINTENANCE COSTS

The age of a building and the condition of a building go hand in hand with the maintenance of the building. The maintenance of the building comes back to the strata manager and the owners committee. If the owners don't agree to charge appropriate strata fees to meet the future needs of the building maintenance, then the strata manager will struggle to do their job. When a building is mainly owned by investors who don't visit the building on a regular basis, they may not appreciate how quickly a building can become run-down. If the building looks run-down from the outside, buyers will assume that it is also run-down on the inside – there could be plumbing issues, common area painting, hallway carpets and driveway cracks that need fixing.

### Sold story

I sold a one-bedroom unit in a building of four units where the building itself was in dire need of maintenance. The roofline bargeboards and all the wooden window frames were bare, with the paint peeled off. They needed to be stripped and primed and painted, but to do this the building would need to be scaffolded for the painter. The cost of delivering and installing the scaffold on a two- or three-storey building is often higher than the price to paint, but you can't paint without the scaffold. The four owners managed the building themselves and had not saved enough through their managed contributions to afford the work, so it didn't get done. The window frames were subject to dry rot and the rain got in around the glass. The building looked like no-one cared about it, which made the sale of one unit more difficult than it should have been. The buyer was concerned about the lack of maintenance and the cost to bring it back to an acceptable level. As there was no money available in the capital works fund and some owners were unable to contribute, it is still an ongoing issue today.

The current condition of a building will affect the sale price of individual units. When repairs and maintenance are required but there is no money available then the owners will need to consider a special levy: that is, to require all owners to pay an extraordinary payment to cover the cost of the repairs.

## Sold story

I sold a one-bedroom apartment in a large building. While the building was reasonably managed, the owners needed to address the issue of balcony rail height requirements, which have increased over the years. The existing balcony rails were lower than the current code so they needed to be raised or replaced. The owners agreed to replace the old balcony railings with new glass railings and so the unit I was selling came with a $21,000 special levy which the current owner could not pay. The unit was being sold because the owner could not afford to make the apartment safe. The sale price included the agreement that the new purchaser would pay the special levy, but it was not included in the purchase price or it would have been subject to stamp duty.

It is not uncommon for owners, particularly those who have been in a unit for a decade or two or three, to be unable to pay special levies. Another one-bedroom unit which I sold had a $50,000 special levy to replace the balcony rail and change the aluminium sliding door of the balcony to a bifold door. When the owner can't afford the levy, it's effectively a forced sale and, depending on the agent selling the unit, the buyer may purchase the apartment below market value just to get the deal done.

## Asbestos containing materials

Some older unit buildings may have a small white sign displayed near the entrance with the words: 'This building contains ACM'. What does this mean and is it a concern? ACM stands for asbestos containing materials, which identifies that the building includes materials with more than 1 per cent asbestos.

When buyers hear the word 'asbestos', they generally panic. They only know the bad news stories they have seen on TV that include the word 'asbestos'. However, just because a building has been identified as containing ACM doesn't mean it's a bad buy. The asbestos referred to may be contained in building materials of the era which are part and parcel of the building structure, with which residents are unlikely to come into any day-to-day contact.

It is a useful sign for tradesmen attending the building to be aware of the ACM. Asbestos fibres are almost indestructible, which makes them durable, so they were often combined with other materials in thousands of products in the building industry – including insulation, fireproofing, decorative plaster, cement pipe, sheet materials, tiles, wallboards, siding and roofing including vermiculite ceilings. A common product in years gone by that may or may not contain asbestos is 'fibro', used in almost every building of the day as the underside of eaves and as sheeting in bathrooms. If in doubt, you can test a building material for the presence of asbestos by mailing a suitably packaged sample to a test laboratory for analysis. Check online for details of a testing laboratory near you.

## Concrete spalling

In my local area, many older buildings, particularly near the coast, have either current concrete spalling or a history of treating concrete spalling over many years. Sometimes referred to as 'concrete cancer' by overdramatic buyers, spalling is caused when water and sometimes salt enters a concrete slab and causes the steel reinforcing within the slab to rust and expand. As the steel expands, the concrete around it cracks and may pop up like a blister, causing a lump under the carpet or flooring of a unit. This may be the first sign to the owner that concrete spalling is present in their unit.

Concrete spalling is not the end of the world and, as it is so common, there are plenty of treatments available to remedy it, at a cost. It's a strata issue, not a cost for the individual owner. If the strata committee have dealt with concrete spalling in the past, there will be mention of it in the strata meeting minutes, so it's always advisable to read these, either by arrangement at the strata manager's office or in a strata report.

I don't know of any instances in which a bank has refused to lend on an apartment where concrete spalling is present, as it is very manageable and treatable. However, I have known buyers who don't understand spalling who will not go ahead with a purchase if a building has a history of concrete spalling. It's very much a case of buyer beware: do your homework before purchase.

## Sold story

I sold a unit in Neutral Bay in a building with a known history of concrete spalling. It is in a harbourside location and subject to salt breezes and coastal rains. The building has about 60 units and only a few had been identified as having concrete spalling. The owner suggested that it was caused by the tenant leaving the balcony door open during a storm so that the rainwater wet the carpet inside the unit, which in turn leached into the concrete floor; some time later, the steel rusted and the concrete floor popped up in places. The owners corporation was notified, it was recorded in the minutes of the committee meetings and some funds were allocated from the sinking fund to attend to the problem at the appropriate time. The committee decided against checking every unit, as it would mean pulling up the carpets and floors of all the units, many of which were leased. Instead, they scheduled repairs to those units that found the issue themselves and waited for other owners to pull up their own floor coverings when they were updating. Over time, they will inspect all unit floors and fix them accordingly. This course of action was acceptable to the buyer of the unit and despite 'concrete cancer' the sale went ahead. A level-headed approach seems to deflect initial alarmist concerns. That said, it will be an issue for some buyers who don't want to know about it or deal with it.

# PETS

This is a deal-breaker for many buyers. If they can't bring their cat or dog with them, then they don't want to live in the building. Many buyers will suggest that owners who don't allow a cat or a dog would be happier people if they had a cat or a dog themselves. They also say that if they are not allowed to have their pet, what sort of neighbours could they expect to have? People who don't tolerate pets!

Some strata committees have introduced their own by-law to specifically ban the keeping of pets in their building. As an example, I read a by-law recently in a contract of sale that was along these lines:

***Special By-Law 7 – Keeping of animals***

*Definition and Interpretation*

*1.  In this by-law:*

    *a)  Act means the* Strata Schemes Management Act 2015.

b) *'Assistance Animal' has the meaning attributed to that expression in the* Disability Discrimination Act 1992.

c) *'Permitted Animal' means a cat or a dog approved by the strata committee.*

2. *Pets Policy – An owner or an occupier must not keep any animal in the strata scheme unless the animal is an Assistance Animal or a Permitted Animal.*

The by-law specified the need to provide evidence that an animal is an Assistance Animal. If evidence was not provided, the strata committee could issue a Breach Notice and, if necessary, a Pet Eviction Notice in accordance with this by-law. The by-law also addressed additional breaches, indemnity, costs associated with cleaning fees, strata managing agents' fees and legal costs.

Some buildings will vary non-application of their by-laws. For instance, they may allow an existing older pet, like a 12-year-old house cat that lives inside, only for the duration of its natural life. This means the buyer can move into the apartment with their companion animal; however, when the cat dies, they can't replace it with another animal. Some committees may allow cats but not dogs; one contract I have seen even had a by-law enforced to the effect that 'the keeping of fish is permitted so long as the fish is in a suitable container'.

Buildings which have no existing by-laws prohibiting the keeping of animals will usually mention this in the contract of sale, with a statement along the lines of, 'The keeping of animals is permitted on successful application to the strata committee, where no unreasonable request will be denied'. This usually means that the buyer needs to work with the real estate agent selling the unit, in advance of the sale, to submit a 'request to keep an animal' application. Such an application includes a full description of the animal, its age and weight and a recent photograph, on which it can be judged 'acceptable'.

### Sold story

I sold an apartment for an owner who had bought into a building with a no-pets policy in place believing that she could change the rules or they would make an exception for her. Unfortunately, it didn't go her way and after months of confrontation she decided that her dog was more important than the people in the building, so selling was the best solution.

Even if you are not a pet-owner yourself, by purchasing a unit where residents are not permitted to have pets, you are limiting the pool of potential purchasers when you decide to sell the property.

# OUTDOOR AREAS

One of the reasons people love a freestanding house is because it offers them outside space to call their own. Similarly, when it comes to units, outdoor space is highly sought after. It comes in different shapes and sizes, with the most common outdoor area being a balcony, which may be open or covered. It may have a view or aspect or it may look straight into another property, but if you can put a table and chairs on it and entertain on it, then it's your own outdoor area, no matter what size it is.

## BALCONIES

Most buyers tell me they want a balcony, however I continue to be able to sell units without balconies, once I have found the right buyer. There is always a buyer who is not concerned about whether the unit has a balcony or not, probably because not all balconies are useable all year round. It's worth remembering that the higher the building, the windier it may be and if it is facing south then that wind can be very cold in winter, so the balcony is almost out of bounds for a quarter of the year.

## Sold story

I sold a two-bedroom unit, a third-storey walk-up (68 stairs) with a half-covered car space, because the buyer loved the north-facing balcony off the living room, which let sunshine into the apartment all day long. It was a relatively small balcony at 10 m², which meant it only fit a small, round table, two café-style chairs and a pot plant, but it was sunny. There was no district view, although the balcony was higher than the building next door – the outlook from the balcony was of the roof next door, a large mass of dark concrete tiles with a skylight in it. The buyer liked the fact that the balcony door could be left open, for sun and a breeze, and no-one could break in as it was on the third floor. The balcony was only big enough to accommodate two people seated for a morning coffee or an evening pinot noir. But that's all the buyer wanted, a little balcony to call their own.

There are a lot of units that were built in the 1960s and 1970s that don't have balconies or any outside space. Often the buildings were built at the same time in the same street by the same builder and they tended to keep each building pretty much the same. It's a lot easier to sell a unit without a balcony when none of the surrounding units have balconies either.

When I am selling a unit without a balcony it's usually the men rather than the women who comment that they must have a balcony, often because they want to have a barbecue. However, not all strata buildings allow barbecues on balconies and many have by-laws against smoking on balconies due to smoke-drift. Individual strata schemes will have their own by-laws; some may have voted for 100 per cent smoke-free while others permit smoking only in designated areas, so be sure to check the by-laws.

## Sold story

I sold a unit which was one of two in the building which did not have a balcony. I don't know why the two units did not have balconies when all the others did. However, the buyer's father was a builder and he could imagine buying the unit and adding a balcony. There was no guarantee that he could add the balcony, but once the buyer had purchased the unit, the father discussed his ideas with a structural engineer, then met with the owners corporation and presented his case, which had no detrimental effect on any other owner or their unit. As you might expect with a committee, not everyone was in favour of the balcony but, at the end of the day, his application was approved, and they have since built the balcony. They changed the windows to doors for access and in the process added substantial value to the property, as well as increasing the day-to-day enjoyment of the property. This man had the vision and saw it through for a win. Have you got the vision to add value?

## Sold story

I sold a one-bedroom apartment in a building completed in 1964. Each apartment had a modest balcony of about 8 m$^2$ with a door opening onto it from the living room. I was told by the owner that when they were being constructed, the builder offered buyers the option of retaining the balcony in its original configuration or choosing to have part of the balcony enclosed with aluminium windows and reducing the outside balcony to 2 m$^2$. The apartment I sold had the modified balcony, although the original strata plan with the full-size balcony was in the contract. Other owners who inspected during the sale said that the modified balcony was the better option as it gave the apartment 6 m$^2$ of extra internal space and the outside balcony was too windy to use anyway.

## COMMUNAL GARDENS

The alternative to a balcony unit may be a ground floor unit, which in many older-style buildings may offer some garden or courtyard access. However, this outside space is usually part of the common area, which means it is not on title for the unit and can be used by any resident in the building. It also means you can't fence it or build on it or even leave your own outdoor furniture there unless agreed to by the other owners who will also make use of it.

External common areas with garden or a courtyard may lend themselves to being a residents' 'meeting place' with table and chairs and perhaps a barbecue or vegetable garden. This is probably the most valuable space available to the resident of a one-bedroom unit, as it gives you an alternate space to go to, particularly if you wish to invite a few friends over and your unit is simply too small.

Unit residents who have direct access onto common property often assume their own form of ownership of the garden because it is rarely used by owners living upstairs. They may even approach the other owners in the building to request a by-law allowing them 'exclusive use' of part of the garden in return for guaranteed maintenance of it or, in some cases, a fee for use of the space. This agreement would allow that owner exclusive use so that it is no longer common property, but it is not on the individual unit property title either. I have seen small hedges planted to differentiate 'exclusive use' from 'common property', which act as a fence where no fence can be built. Garden units are in strong demand for both couples planning to have a child in the near future and downsizers who have given up a garden but still want to potter around in some green space.

I have seen common areas turned into communal vegetable gardens by enthusiastic residents – which benefits the whole building – and other common areas made into clothes-drying areas, with outdoor clothes lines adjacent to ground-floor shared laundries. Older buildings may also have a 'gardener's loo' on the ground floor, to provide facilities for the gardeners who maintain the common area.

## COMMUNAL ROOFTOPS

Some buildings also offer communal terrace areas at the entrance, where residents can gather to enjoy some open space, and some buildings have a common rooftop viewing area where residents can take in the view or fireworks on special nights. These areas are often locked so they have restricted access, to ensure safety, and rarely do they have seating or tables, which may blow over the edge unless they are bolted down.

Many new apartment buildings are embracing the rooftop area and providing residents with a range of entertainment facilities from pools and gyms to bars and cinemas. Sydney buildings have over the decades ignored roof terraces, making roofs no-go zones, even though they may offer harbour views or a safe and open space; instead, they house air-conditioning units and the lift-well maintenance equipment. The rooftop of the unit building you are considering may be an opportunity to add value for all owners, if someone is able to encourage the owners corporation to embrace the space.

# 12

# OUTLOOK AND ASPECT

When you buy a unit, you can't change the outlook or the aspect. Buyers of units are generally looking for a place with some sort of an outlook and a sunny aspect.

## LIGHT

While I have sold many units that will never see a ray of sunshine through their window, it's a big buyer objection when the unit gets no sun at all. Buyers want a northerly aspect because they expect sun all day. An easterly aspect gives them the morning sun, while a westerly aspect always raises complaints over 'how hot it will be in summer' – but no-one ever complains about 'how lovely the westerly sun is in winter'. The last choice for buyers is the southerly aspect, which offers very little direct sun.

Of course, while it's preferable to have a northerly aspect, if the high-rise building next door to your north blocks the sun all day and your outlook is, in fact, 12 neighbours looking back at you, perhaps the south side of the building with the tree outlook is a better buy.

> ## Sold story
>
> I sold an elevated ground floor apartment with a north-facing balcony that got lots of lovely sun, but the outlook was a laneway with an old paling fence and the apartment was just above street level, so you could almost jump up and climb in. Some buyers didn't feel safe. They may not have even noticed that adjacent to the balcony, in the laneway, was the double-width electric roller door to the garage, which rattled up and down every time a resident's car or motorbike came and went, at any time of the day and night. Motor scooters are not too bad, but some motorbikes can be very noisy.

## VIEWS

There are hundreds of units with no outlook. They literally look straight into another unit or look at a brick wall or fence or, worse, an illuminated sign.

> ## Sold story
>
> I sold a million-dollar unit where the outlook was the back of some old shops covered in graffiti and the aspect was southerly, overlooking the main road, but the most prominent view from the living room was the enormous illuminated golden arches sign of a McDonald's restaurant which trades 24/7, so it is never turned off. I remember a buyer who inspected the apartment; she was a personal trainer and she told me that there wasn't a chance in the world that she would ever buy this apartment, as her friends and co-workers would never stop laughing at her.

As a real estate agent, when I am invited to appraise a unit, I consider the aspect and views in terms of colours. How much brown, green and blue can I see? I consider brown to be anything that is not green or blue: roofs, buildings, signage, car parks and so on. Green is good – it's foliage, trees, grass, parks, anything that is not brown or blue. Blue is all about the money: how much blue water is in the outlook? Does the property have a water view? Does the water view make you say, 'Wow'?

The question buyers always ask is, 'How much is a water view worth?' The answer is always this: it's worth different amounts to different people. If you have enjoyed a great water view from your apartment, you will know it is very hard to give up. You will also know it is very hard to quantify the emotion that a water view provides as a dollar figure. If a buyer has a choice, they will stretch to buy a property with a view, especially if it is a blue view.

# 13

# ACCESS AND SECURITY

Buyers like good building access. Units that don't have level street access are less desirable than those that do and can be marked hard. If I show a buyer two units, one of which has a level concrete path from the street entrance to the front door of the building and the other has steps from the street and multiple levels before arriving at the front door of the building, the level-access property is the preferred option. There will be a price difference that is difficult to avoid.

Some buildings are just in difficult locations. Buildings on hills or the sides of ridges create challenges. Access from the car parking is also a big factor. Imagine the buyer coming home with a child or simply the groceries, parking their car and then struggling up and down just to get to the front door of the building. Buyers prefer direct access from the car park to the building, preferably to a lift that takes them directly to their floor. Even better is direct access to their unit from the car park. I have sold many townhouse-style properties that have a single car space with a door providing direct access via stairs to the apartment.

Safe access goes hand in hand with security. Buyers like to feel that their home is their sanctuary, so it must be safe. At a minimum that means excellent lighting and that the building front door is locked at all times, so no-one can just wander in. Many older-style buildings were not built this way; they may have been upgraded or may provide the opportunity to upgrade. Buyers are security conscious and every layer of security gives them reassurance that this is the right apartment for them.

## INTERCOMS AND LIFT FOBS

Buyers like restricted access in a large building, which involves having a programmed key fob system that limits residents' access to their own floor only. This means that if you live on level 3, you can't access level 4 or any other floor. These key fobs may also keep a record of who comes and goes from the building and at what time.

Buyers also like video intercom access. Audio-only intercom is better than no intercom, but video is much preferred. It allows residents to see who just rang their bell and decide if they will allow them in or not. This type of access is also important for visitors to the building, especially those who may be parking in the visitor section of the car park.

## CCTV

The next level of security is CCTV (Closed Circuit Television) and many buildings have now fitted this as a security measure, particularly in and around the letterboxes, which may be targeted by thieves looking for credit cards and account information. CCTV is a good deterrent as it provides pictures on a timeline in case of any incident, which may be invaluable to police in tracking down troublemakers.

## A CONCIERGE

The highest level of security includes all the items we have discussed plus a part-time or full-time building concierge, who monitors and manages everyone who comes and goes in the building. While concierge services are an expense, they are a genuine luxury that the right buyers will pay for and the cost is often outweighed by the value that a friendly face provides. It's easy to see the cost of a concierge in your strata fees, however the value of the concierge is much harder to quantify.

# BUILDING FACILITIES

An apartment building's facilities have a big impact on how desirable the apartments are. Basics like laundry facilities, hot water services and rubbish arrangements are key, but lifestyle facilities can also sway a buyer towards or away from a property. The cost of maintaining these increases the owner's strata fees, so there are pros and cons.

## LAUNDRY FACILITIES

Most older-style buildings were not built with laundry facilities inside the unit. Instead, they may have a common area laundry room, either on the ground floor, or one per floor depending on the size of the building.

The strata committee may allow individual residents to install their own washing machine and perhaps a dryer and provide them with an individual power point per unit so that their electricity is charged straight back to their unit account. Power points are sometimes protected from use by other residents by a padlocked cover. Often there is not enough space for all residents to have their own machines, in which case the owners corporation may contract out the supply of two or more commercial washing machines and dryers to an outside supplier. These are then provided for all residents to use on a first come, first served basis and are either coin-operated, to help with costs, or are paid for from the owners' quarterly contributions.

Often older buildings will have an outdoor Hills Hoist clothes line or two in a courtyard, particularly if dryers are not supplied for residents. Some progressive older buildings have installed extension-style clothes lines in an undercover common area in a bid to provide 'all weather' protection.

The downside of shared laundries is their location. They are often tucked away under a building on the ground floor, or in the basement, which means residents need to cart their dirty washing down to the laundry only to find that someone beat them to it and all the machines are being used. These laundries are rarely locked, so leaving your washing unattended may not be a good idea.

The alternative to shared laundries is dedicated internal laundries in each unit or modifying the bathroom space to fit a washing machine and possibly dryer of your own. If space is tight, you may be able to fit a front-loader or a combination washer/dryer machine under the bench. Naturally the washing machine needs to be plumbed to water, which is why the bathroom is often the first choice. However, if the space still won't allow, the other option is an under-bench front-loader in the kitchen area. While buyers prefer to do their own washing and drying of their 'smalls' in the privacy of their own unit, the larger washing machines in the shared laundries make the washing of bed sheets a lot easier.

## HOT WATER SERVICE

Depending on their age and size, and whether they have been updated, unit blocks may have different set-ups to provide hot water to each unit. They can be individual hot water tanks, typically 50 litres in size, which are often located under the kitchen sink and take up quite a bit of space. Some units have individual gas hot water systems which may be mounted on the wall in the bathroom and flued outside. Some units have the hot water storage supply outside on the balcony. If an individual gas unit has been recently replaced, it may have been upgraded to an instantaneous continuous supply unit which heats the water through copper pipes on demand, so you never run out of hot water. Many buyers prefer the control this gives them because everyone fears running out of hot water at the wrong time, so having your own on-demand unit offers peace of mind.

The other option for individual units is a community hot water service. This is often a combination of large electric hot water storage units of 250 litres or 315 litres located in a central area off the garage, which supply hot water to all the units in the building. Some buildings will have a community hot water service in the roof of the building on a gravity feed system. Some buildings divide up the apartments and have two hot water units to service two groups of unit owners.

## GARBAGE ROOM

We all generate rubbish, but it seems in years gone by we generated a lot less – many older buildings don't have a dedicated common-area rubbish room, so the bins may not have their own home. The age of the building and the attitude of its residents will determine the way rubbish is handled at the building. Many multistorey buildings include a garbage chute on each floor for residents to deposit their rubbish in, which feeds to a general waste bin on the ground floor.

Some strata schemes appoint a resident owner as a caretaker, and if it is not a shared volunteer position, then it may be a paid position to manage the day-to-day running of the building, particularly rubbish management. Councils collect bins on a weekly basis, generally, and residents are encouraged to sort rubbish into general waste and waste for recycling, such as cardboard, paper, bottles and containers. If the waste collectors don't come onto the property to collect the bins themselves, the caretakers will likely be responsible for putting out the bins and bringing them in again.

I know of a building where a unit is directly above the garbage bin storage area – and I would not like to sit on that balcony in the height of the summer heat. It's just something to bear in mind: if the garbage bins are already stored in a location that affects your potential unit then it will be very hard to move them, because no other owner is going to agree to have them affect their unit.

There is also a noise factor when bins are collected, which may or may not be an issue for every unit. Garbage trucks generate incredibly intense stop-start engine and hydraulic noise, along with the sound of the broken bottles crashing into the collection pit of the truck. It's another good reason to avoid buying a unit next door to a pub.

## LIFESTYLE FACILITIES

'Lifestyle' building facilities are nice to have but not essential to day-to-day life, and they may come at a cost that is part of the quarterly levies. Such facilities will be in or on common areas, so they are not restricted to any one unit (in which case they would be deemed 'exclusive use').

Some unit buildings have added a gym or recreational area. This can be any building space that can be adapted to a new use. Often it is windowless and may have been used for storage in the past, but by adding some mirrors and an air conditioner, plus some exercise equipment, it can be passed off as a dedicated gym. The owners committee will generally purchase or lease the gym equipment and provide it for residents at no charge, but the costs will still need to be paid from quarterly fees or a special levy. This is most likely the least used space in a building.

Bike storage is more common these days; it may not be too hard to find a place for residents to park and lock a pushbike. If pushbikes are on show to visitors, though, they can easily become a target for thieves, so a secure area is preferable. I know of a building with bike racks undercover near the front door and they are covered by CCTV, nevertheless the bikes that are chained to the rack are still stolen from time to time.

Other building facilities like swimming pools, saunas, steam rooms and cafés are unlikely to be part of the unit-style buildings that we are looking for. It's worth knowing that, while they are part of a modern unit and in some cases add value to the overall attraction of a building, they all come at a cost to the residents. We need to take the line that a buyer looking for that level of 'luxury' will be looking for a larger and more modern building than we are looking for. Older-style buildings rarely provide any of these building facilities at all.

# PARKING AND STORAGE

A unit will either have a lock-up garage, an undercover car space, an open-air car space, 'scramble' parking (first come, first served) or no parking at all. Many older buildings don't have lock-up garages and instead offer one of the other options. In general terms, any parking space is better than no parking space. However, not everyone needs parking – although everyone wants a garage.

## OPEN-AIR PARKING SPACES

The objection to open-air spaces from buyers is always, 'But what if there's hail?' My response is usually something along the lines of, 'It can hail at any time; your car may be stuck in traffic when it hails, not safely at home'. An open-air car space is still a much better option than no space at all.

I have sold units which had five open-air car spaces in a row at the back of the building and the owners corporation agreed to allow those car space owners to pay for their own carport-style roof to be built over the five spaces, which has added value to all those apartments for a shared and minimal cost. When you are looking at properties, always be looking for the upside: what opportunities there are to add value, subject to owners corporation agreement of course.

## GARAGES

Undercover or open-air car spaces are just for cars or bikes. You can't store things in your car space, which is why lock-up garages with individual doors are worth more to many buyers. Garages can be configured inside to hang pushbikes on the wall, hang a kayak from the ceiling and have storage shelves at the back, maybe even a hobby workbench.

Older buyers may have a 'pride and joy' car, so they really want a garage for their car. This is not negotiable for them.

If you are looking at a garage, check to see if it has a light and a power point – both will add value to your resale. You need power in your garage to add a remote-control garage door motor (with a light). An auto door is much more 'luxurious' than having to stop the car, get out of the car, wrestle to open the heavy garage door manually, get back in the car and then park the car and pull the garage door down behind you and make sure it is locked.

## SCRAMBLE SPACES

The other option for unit parking is what I call 'scramble spaces' – these are car spaces on the grounds of the building, usually open-air spaces, which are not allocated or 'on title' or 'exclusive use' to any particular unit. They are available to residents on a first come, first served basis and if you drive away from a space, any other resident can occupy it. Again, it's better than no parking at all.

## CAR STACKERS

Some buildings are suitable for car stackers. That is, you have one car space and you either dig down to store a car or have the height available above to stack one car on top of another. Stackers are more affordable than they used to be and are more common in new apartment buildings now, but they can be retrofitted to suitable older buildings. If a car stacker is a viable solution, it's worth investigating the options available to you.

## NO PARKING

Residents of buildings with limited or no parking may be eligible through their local council for a resident parking permit that allows them to park close to their address for an unlimited period. Usually, they allow one car parking permit per household. If the sign in the street reads something along the lines of, 'Two-hour parking, resident permits excluded', you know this scheme is in place, but it would be worth checking with council to be sure.

If the unit building is close to an inner-city commercial car park, you might also like to look at the cost of contract parking for a reserved space in a commercial car park or investigate other adjoining buildings to see if there are any 'on title' spaces that are not being used by the owner. Not everyone who owns a parking space has a car to park there. For instance, our office building has no parking provided; however, the apartment building next door has allocated parking spaces for all apartments but not all owners have a car. I pay a monthly fee to an owner without a car to occupy their car space on a semi-permanent basis. It gives the owner a bit of spending money and gives me the security of knowing my space is always there. The cost to me is less than a monthly parking ticket so it's a win–win situation for us both. If the owner decided to sell the apartment, I may lose my car space, but the new owner may be just as happy to continue the arrangement.

---

## Sold story

Just as units are called 'lots' on the strata plan, some units have car spaces or garages that are on separate 'lots' as well. I sold a unit that was Lot 53 on the contract of sale, which included Lot 11, a car space in the same building. The two lots were sold together on the one contract such that the unit was sold with parking. However, the owner could have separated the two lots and sold the unit without parking and kept ownership of the car space lot. As a lot, the car space has its own unit entitlement based on size and is subject to strata fees, just as the unit is. In this case, the unit had a quarterly strata fee of $1105 and the car space had a quarterly fee of $28.35. The owner could also have offered to sell the car space lot to another owner in the building as an individual 'lot' sale. This is how a one-bedroom unit owner may come to have two car spaces, which is another way of adding value.

---

## VISITOR PARKING

Most new apartment buildings will also allocate a certain number of visitor parking spaces as part of their original development plans. Most older-style buildings, however, won't have enough parking spaces for each unit to have an on-title space, let alone offer visitor spaces. I have just sold in a new building with 23 apartments which provided secure (under-building, behind a remote access door) individual parking spaces, with five spaces for visitors and one space for car washing, which had its own drainage and tap and hose provided.

Visitor parking spaces often have a sign saying, 'No overnight parking' or giving a time limit for visitors. They are not provided as a second space option for residents and may be policed by other residents in the building who 'keep an eye on things'. You could expect a letter and/or a fine from the owners committee on your first offence.

## Sold story

Buyers are always asking, 'What is the value of a car space in Sydney?' Well, here are some sales that may surprise you. In June 2015, an open-air car space at 29 Carabella Street, Kirribilli, a lot of 12 m$^2$, sold at auction to a local resident for $120,000. The auction reserve was $50,000 and several locals bid to secure the lot, simply for the sake of convenience. In December 2016 a car space lot at 2 Springfield Avenue, Potts Point, sold for $166,000; the same space had previously sold in 2010 for $95,000. In February 2017, a 15 m$^2$ space was sold at 6 Challis Street, Potts Point, for $190,000 to a local resident who was tired of trying to find a car space near their building. Another car space lot in MacLeay Street, Potts Point, had an opening bid of $120,000 and sold in May 2015 for a then-record $264,000. If these numbers make you want to buy a car space as an investment, try this website: www.findacarpark.com.au. It lists car spaces for rent and sale, and at the time of writing there was a tandem car space in a security garage for two cars for sale in Bond Street, Sydney, for $475,000.

## STORAGE

Everyone says they want a garage, when in many cases what they really want is storage: somewhere to put their stuff. Some unit buildings in which I have sold have a communal storage room, which is one large space for which all residents have a key. There, they can store things that they don't need access to all the time, like pushbikes, golf clubs and suitcases. There is no defined area for individual units, it's on a first come, first served basis.

What I have noticed, by the way, is that with communal storage areas, many owners don't know who stored things belong to. There may be, for example, several empty flat-screen TV boxes stored but seemingly not belonging to anyone. Chances are they were put there by tenants who have long since moved out and they left them behind (often deliberately). It's a good idea for the owners corporation to flag an annual clear-out of the storage room, otherwise it just becomes a dumping room. Again, from a buyer's perspective any storage is still better than no storage.

I have also sold units in which the owners corporation has created individual storage rooms for each unit with a key-locked door. These storage areas are often under the main building, behind a set of stairs or behind a laundry in an otherwise 'dead zone'. This type of storage is a bonus for buyers so always check to see if a building offers individual storage; sometimes it is 'on title' for each unit and sometimes it is 'exclusive use' for individual units. Sometimes there is not enough space for everyone to have a dedicated storage unit as they may have been allocated years ago to the owners who created the by-laws regarding the space at the time.

# ABOUT STRATA REPORTS

When you are buying, you should expect the seller to provide an independent strata report for you at no charge. This shows that they are putting all their cards on the table and there is nothing to hide. You need that information to assess the comings and goings in the building. Ask the seller for it if they haven't already provided the report. It is a cost to you to have to source the strata report yourself – and if you don't go ahead with the sale, it's a dead-end cost.

If a buyer short-lists five units and pays for five strata reports, plus the 'spend' on the time it takes to have them compiled by a third party, the agents and sellers are wasting a lot of this buyer's time and money. Buyers are delighted when I offer them a strata report at no charge. They can immediately gain more details about the building and, should they choose to, move forward with an offer based on the information on hand.

If the selling agent is not willing to supply a strata report, then you will need to make your own enquiries with the strata manager. This may take a week, depending on their availability.

The strata report provides all the relevant information you need to be able to assess the building, owners and finances to decide if the building is right for you. Typically, it will cover the following areas:

- strata roll
- common property and strata plan/title search
- model by-laws and special by-laws
- financial accounts/balance sheet
- maintenance levies
- budget and contributions
- standard levies and special levies
- insurances and valuation
- notices and orders/fire statement
- ten-year sinking fund plan
- annual general meeting minutes
- notable items
- building matters
- history of expenditure
- miscellaneous items.

You should read through the report and obtain advice about anything that concerns you. Take special note of the by-laws – especially any special by-laws about renovations and improvements – the comparative apartment pricing provided and the expenses.

## BY-LAWS

The special by-laws may include reference to past topics that were raised and discussed, and their specific outcomes. For example, an owner may have approached the strata committee to request installing an exterior awning to serve the balcony on their lot. The committee decided whether they were in favour and what conditions related to the request, then recorded these conditions as a by-law. For instance, the conditions may have included: the awning must be charcoal in colour, have supporting anodised arms, use non-fade sun-safe material, be square-edge flap in style and retractable or vertical in design, and the cost of installation and maintenance of any installed awning will be the responsibility of the individual lot owner.

By-laws in relation to renovations may be grouped under a special by-law, such as 'Building works', and will include definitions, written notice requirements to the owners corporation, scope of works and evidence that they do not require council permission or that council permission has been obtained. Additional by-laws will detail the requirements for 'Undertaking building works', 'The building works' themselves and 'After the works', plus clauses on maintenance, damage, bond, indemnity, insurance and costs.

## COMPARATIVE AND SQUARE METRE PRICING

Units and apartments in a single building that have recently sold will provide you with a comparative price basis in the strata report, depending on their level of renovation and presentation. For instance, the sales in the case study building we'll be looking at in chapter 18, at 6–8 Hardie Street, Neutral Bay, NSW, (see table overleaf) help us to determine the next price expectations of the agent and the owner for a future sale.

| Property | Size | Date sold | Condition | Sale price | $ per m² |
|----------|------|-----------|-----------|------------|----------|
| Unit 24 | 44 m² | Feb 2019 | Updated | $620,000 | $14,090 |
| Unit 23 | 50 m² | Dec 2018 | Unrenovated | $635,000 | $12,700 |
| Unit 27 | 44 m² | Nov 2018 | Updated | $650,000 | $14,772 |
| Unit 9 | 44 m² | Oct 2017 | Renovated | $690,000 | $15,681 |
| Unit 26 | 44 m² | Aug 2017 | Updated | $686,000 | $15,590 |
| Unit 18 | 50 m² | Dec 2016 | Renovated | $690,000 | $13,800 |

When you divide the sale price by the square metreage you will get the price per square metre, which is a benchmark price when comparing one apartment with another. Obviously, whether the unit is original, updated (meaning there's been a change of some fixtures) or renovated throughout, and the date it sold are important criteria to consider. Unit 23, our subject unit in the case study, was purchased by investors at the lowest per square metre rate of all the sales in the building over a three-year period. This shows that the purchasers bought well and there is scope to add value, with other units in the building selling for considerably more per square metre.

## STRATA EXPENSES

In New South Wales, the owners corporation is required to maintain a ten-year plan of expected major expenditure and set the owners' quarterly contributions at a level at which these items will be able to be funded, without a special levy. A typical small building with a mix of one- and two-bedroom units may include the following expense categories in its ten-year capital works forecast:

- roof
- long-term capital items
- common property doors
- common property lighting
- elevators and equipment
- timberwork
- fire safety
- guttering and downpipes
- garage door motor
- waterproofing
- ventilation
- hot water system
- internal painting
- carpet
- intercom
- floor tiles
- hydraulic pump
- external painting
- landscaping
- fences
- retaining walls
- sealing concrete areas

- trip hazards
- storm water drains
- storm water pumps
- skylights
- line marking
- windows.

This is not an exhaustive list, but it gives you an idea of the typical items that may be covered to reflect the individual needs of each building. I recommend you get further information on what's required in relation to strata expense planning in your state or territory – see appendix A for some helpful links.

# 17

# WHAT TO LOOK FOR IN A CONTRACT OF SALE

In this chapter, I refer to New South Wales contracts, as I know them well; the information in contracts in other states and territories may be in a different order or format, but will be largely similar.

By the time you're looking at a contract of sale, you have a special interest in the property. If you have specific questions, it's best to ask the conveyancer who is representing you so that you understand the way things are done in your state or territory.

Every property needs a contract of sale in order to change hands and strata properties are no different. In fact, a contract of sale can often run to over 100 pages, particularly if the buildings have a long history of by-laws, litigation and maintenance. In addition, if the property has a tenant then a full copy of the tenancy agreement is also included in the contract of sale. As a buyer, you will appoint a property conveyancer to represent the purchase and negotiation of the contract, to exchange of contracts and through to settlement. Your conveyancer will be up to date with all relevant changes in legislation affecting strata properties and what to expect and not expect to see within the contract of sale.

Much of a contract of sale will be standard clauses. However, as a flipper you will need to take particular note of the by-laws and special conditions for any restrictions or onerous rules that may affect your ability to renovate and flip.

Note that the contract of sale is not the same thing as a strata report. The contract of sale is the final say; it represents the rules of the building to which all owners are obliged to adhere. The strata report outlines the day-to-day activities within the building, the harmony of the owners and whether they are playing by the rules or not. The contract of sale is required to buy the property, whereas often the strata report will determine if you want to buy the property or not.

## STANDARD AND SPECIAL PROVISIONS

Contracts in New South Wales will likely be provided as the *Contract for Sale and Purchase of Land*, which has standard provisions usually of about 13 pages, with 31 main clauses and their subclauses. This is followed by special conditions and amendments to the contract, which are prepared by the conveyancer creating the contract of sale. The next section is called 'Strata title property requisitions on title', with some 30 questions and replies to requisitions specifically relating to the purchase of strata title property. The contract of sale will then provide title search information.

## THE STRATA PLAN

The next section is the strata plan, which provides the property details in a survey form. This consists of a site drawing and orientation, then a drawing of each building floor and the individual lots, including parking and common areas such as lifts and stairwells, storage spaces and amenities. The strata plan also provides unit entitlement and surveyed size for each unit and the strata plan registration date. This is all valuable information to help you understand the position of the unit of interest to you in relation to the other units in the building.

## STANDARD STRATA CLAUSES

The next contract section, in a New South Wales contract, may be Schedule 2 of the Strata Schemes Management Regulation 2016, 'By-laws for pre-1996 strata schemes'. These are the 19 standard clauses in relation to strata properties that include subjects such as noise, obstruction, damage, behaviour, rubbish, drying, cleaning, storage, use of common property, floor coverings and keeping of animals.

## BY-LAWS ABOUT RENOVATING

The contract of sale may then provide any changes to the by-laws that may affect what you can and can't do in terms of renovation and how you go about it. I am looking at a contract of sale at the time of writing that includes a 93-page section headed 'Consolidation/Change of By-Laws under the *Strata Schemes Management Act 2015* and the *Real Property Act 1900*'. Many of these by-laws relate to one form of renovation or another, so, while this may be an extreme example, you may also find it is more common than you first thought. Again, buyer beware – read the contract of sale and ask your conveyancer for advice in relation to what you want to do with the property.

This particular contract of sale then discusses the addition of a special by-law: Renovations. Under the heading of 'Definitions and interpretation', the contract of sale includes the definitions of different types of renovations:

*Cosmetic Work – means an owner's work which affects the common property in connection with their lot for the following purposes:*

- *Installing or replacing nails, hooks, screws and the like for hanging pictures and decorations and other things on the walls, replacing handrails, undertaking painting and the filling of minor holes and cracks in internal walls, carpet laying, installing or replacing built-in wardrobes, replacing internal blinds or curtains, changing locks or safety devices and insect or animal screens.*

Additionally, there are clauses relating to 'minor renovations' – meaning an owner's work which affects common property in connection with their lot for the following purposes:

a. *Renovating any room in a lot*
b. *Making changes to recessed light fittings*
c. *Making changes to any wood or other hard floors, lifting carpet to expose hard floors*
d. *Making changes to wiring, pipes, ducts or cabling*
e. *Making changes to power points or access points*
f. *Making changes by reconfiguring any walls*

It goes on to discuss work involving structural changes; work that changes the external appearance of a lot; work that affects safety and fire systems, waterproofing, plumbing or exhaust systems, air conditioning, double-glazed windows, hot water services, skylights or other work that requires additional consent or approval under any other legislation.

A further clause states that 'major renovations' are defined as work that is not 'cosmetic work' or 'minor renovations', which pretty much covers everything else. That said, another clause states that an owner may carry out cosmetic work without the approval of the owners corporation as long as they comply with the conditions of the by-laws.

The by-law then defines how an owner must carry out cosmetic work:

*Proper, timely, skilful, workmanlike, with suitable materials, that contractors are adequately supervised, that work is to applicable Australian Standards and the Building Code of Australia, suitable access is provided and contractor parking requirements.*

It also outlines restrictions on when noisy building activities, such as drilling or constant hammering, can be undertaken and the hours of operation of machinery – on weekdays only and excluding public holidays. There is a clause on transportation of construction materials and protecting the strata building from damage, removing all rubbish on a daily basis and ensuring the security of the strata building is not compromised. Furthermore, the owner indemnifies the owners corporation against an exhaustive list of works and situations.

Importantly, there is a clause to the effect that an owner may only carry out minor renovations with the approval of the owners corporation. The owner needs to submit an application in writing including full details of who, what and where; plans, specifications, drawings, conditions and notes; an estimate of the duration and times of the work; details of contractors and labourers; and rubbish removal arrangements, at a minimum. The owners corporation may request additional information, engage a consultant to review the application, impose a conditional approval or refuse the application, but must not act unreasonably when doing so.

## INSURANCE CLAUSES ABOUT RENOVATING

Naturally, the contract of sale also has clauses relating to insurance to ensure that any tradesperson is licensed, insured and covered under law. Other clauses are about the suitability of hard floors and their acoustic certification and rating. The owners corporation may also ask for a structural engineer's report, a waterproofing expert's approval and a dilapidation report and request a bond to be paid, within reason.

The owners corporation will also require notice on completion of the works and access for their nominated inspector. They may also require a post-works dilapidation report prior to returning the bond. You will likely find that an owner is responsible for all costs, fees and expenses incurred by the owners corporation in considering or granting your approval, in relation to a minor renovation.

## MAJOR RENOVATIONS

The by-laws then detail the clauses relating to major renovations by an owner, which follow similar pathways to minor renovations. However, the owner must start with an application to the owners corporation, which is then passed as a special resolution in accordance with the New South Wales *Strata Schemes Management Act 2015* and Strata Schemes Management Regulation 2016 and may incorporate additional conditions set out within the by-laws and accompanying schedules. This may not apply in all states and territories, so ask your conveyancer for their advice. It's fair to say that, depending on the scope of work you are planning, you will be required to jump through many hoops and 'dot every i and cross every t' before you can start any work at all.

Importantly, it is unlikely you will be able to get a start on the paperwork with the owners corporation during the standard six-week settlement period from exchange of contracts to settlement. Many owners corporations simply will not recognise an owner or their applications to undertake renovations until such time as they are officially an owner, which is after settlement.

## COMMON PROPERTY

The by-laws may also contain a Common Property Memorandum detailing the scope of the owners corporation's responsibilities for maintenance, repair and replacement of common property. In the contract of sale I am reviewing, for instance, the scope of common property extends to balconies and courtyards, ceilings and roofs, electrics, the entrance door, floors and general areas, parking and garages plus plumbing and windows.

Equally, it has been decided that the lot owner will be responsible for maintenance, repair or replacement of an extensive list of items that are outside the scope of works that are deemed common property.

## ZONING

The contract of sale then includes the Section 10.7 Planning Certificate provided by the local council under the New South Wales *Environmental Planning and Assessment Act 1979*. Importantly, this document states the zoning for the property, which in this case could be either R2 low-density residential, R3 medium-density residential or R4 high-density residential.

The 10.7 may also include current council planning proposals and proposed amendments such as changes to floor square ratios, changes to maximum heights for development sites under a specific size and proposals specific to planning controls on a current address. This document may also include references to development control plans, infrastructure, heritage controls and other controls such as land acquisition by a public authority and any order under the *Trees (Disputes between Neighbours) Act 2006*.

Lastly, the contract of sale will provide a sewer service diagram for the site.

As contracts vary from state to state and territory to territory, please make your own enquiries regarding zoning in your area. It's important to understand what the property is currently zoned for and what it could potentially be re-zoned for, which could add significant value for owners.

## THE INCLUSIONS

On the front page of the contract of sale is a section with tick boxes for the 'inclusions' and the 'exclusions' for the sale.

When purchasing your unit to upgrade, it is unlikely that much will be included; after all, we are looking for properties that need renovations to flip, not properties that are already updated. The contract will still have a section for the inclusions so it's worth checking that they are ticked if any of the items are physically present. You will probably have some old carpet, old blinds and maybe some curtains, probably no flyscreens or built-in wardrobes, but maybe a stove and a range hood and some type of light fittings. The inclusions itemised should be present but there is no obligation for them to be in working order or even good condition. You are unlikely to keep any of these original items for your upgrade so it really doesn't matter if they work or not – although if they are working you may be able to sell them off on Gumtree (www.gumtree.com.au) or give them away, which saves the cost of taking them to landfill.

## 18

# NEUTRAL BAY CASE STUDY

Now that we've covered the fundamentals of choosing a suitable property, I am going to share with you the details of a unit that I sold in December 2018 in Hardie Street, Neutral Bay, NSW. It's an ideal example of the type of unit you might be able to find to renovate. It ticks many of the boxes we've already talked about as being desirable.

You may be able to find images in the public domain by searching the apartment address in your preferred search engine.

Let's start by looking at the elements we've covered in earlier chapters in relation to this building.

## LOCATION

Unit 23, 6–8 Hardie Street, Neutral Bay, is in a quiet residential street with locals only traffic. It is 500 metres' easy walking distance to Military Road, Neutral Bay and the city bus to Wynyard station in Sydney. It is well positioned to enjoy all the local restaurant/café facilities plus the Oaks Hotel. It has easy access to Coles supermarket and the Big Bear shopping centre. It is adjacent to Neutral Bay Public School and 500 metres walking distance to the popular Neutral Bay Club, which provides tennis courts, lawn bowls and a social bar and bistro plus function rooms. This is next to the popular Ilbery Reserve, which has children's playground equipment. As far as neighbours go, it's a residential street with established units and apartments.

## SIZE AND FLOOR PLAN

The unit is 50 m² and the car space is 14 m² and they are on separate lots.

An initial look at the floor plan suggests it can be improved. The front door opens into a small hallway with the living room to the left and bedroom to the right. The bathroom with internal laundry is off the bedroom. The kitchen is beyond the living room. There are two balconies, one each coming off the living room and bedroom. There may be some scope to move the door for the bathroom to the hallway, so access is not through the bedroom. There may be a possibility of opening up the kitchen wall into the living room. These look to be two structural changes that, if they are possible, will add value.

## THE BUILDING

The strata building was registered in June 1975 and is a blonde-brick seven-storey building with balconies and car parking under the building, with level access from the street.

There are 34 units in the building: 31 are one-bedroom units, 2 are two-bedroom units and 1 is a three-bedroom penthouse.

## FEES AND MAINTENANCE

The fees are in line with other buildings of this age:

- water rates (based on usage): $178.11 per quarter

- council rates: $242.63 per quarter

- strata rates: administration fee $522.30 per quarter plus capital works fund $537.85 per quarter, for a combined amount of $1060.15 per quarter.

The balance in the combined funds at time of enquiry was $204,689.92, which is an average of $6020.29 for each of the 34 units – a healthy situation.

Generally, it's a well-maintained building, with an active strata manager with a ten-year plan. The lift was recently replaced and paid for without a special levy. There are no apparent issues and no special levies.

No signage about asbestos containing materials has been sighted, and there is no known history of concrete spalling in the building.

## PETS

There is no specific by-law against dogs or cats in place, so any application made to strata management will be dealt with on an individual basis with no unreasonable request denied. There are currently owners with pets in the building.

## OUTDOOR AREAS

This apartment has two balconies, and the common area has low maintenance gardens with some seating. There is no rooftop terrace or common area.

## OUTLOOK AND ASPECT

This unit is located on the fourth level in the centre of the building and has unobstructed open views of the Sydney Harbour Bridge across to Chatswood – a sweeping panoramic outlook. The unit faces west. There are north-facing units which look toward another high-rise and there are south facing units which do not get any direct sun. The westerly aspect of this unit means it has direct sun in the afternoons.

## ACCESS AND SECURITY

There is a level pathway from the street to the front door of the building through the gardens or direct access from the car park via the elevator. The car park has a remote-controlled security gate and there is audio-only intercom access to the building by remote front door release. The building has one lift which (as was noted earlier) was replaced in the past 12 months and was fully paid for from owners' contributions.

## BUILDING FACILITIES

There is a large shared laundry on the car park level with washing machines and dryers supplied by strata. There is an individual electric hot water service under the kitchen bench. The garbage room is located in the garage area of the building, so it is out of sight and smell.

There are no common-area 'lifestyle' facilities other than the gardens around the building.

## PARKING

This apartment has an open-air car space on a separate lot on the same title as the unit lot. It is 14 m², which is average size. There are other unit holders who have enclosed their car spaces with walls and a remote-control garage door within the car parking area.

## SPECIAL BY-LAWS

As discussed in chapters 16 and 17, it's important to check the special by-laws. In this instance, the contract of sale contains an annexure that details a special privilege granted to Unit 33/ Lot 33 (which is a two-bedroom unit with a total area of 115 m²) to allow it to be converted for use as two one-bedroom units.

There is approval to make alterations and additions consistent with drawings provided by an architect firm for the construction of a dividing wall in the living/dining room and balcony by removal of the internal walls and the creation of new openings, with fittings, fixtures, electrical, gas, drainage and other services required for use of the lot as two one-bedroom apartments.

There are conditions attached regarding provision of a construction certificate from North Sydney Council and all conditions of approval, plus insurance and liability and a bank guarantee of $20,000 to the owners corporation for a period of six months. Additional clauses apply, such as provision of approvals from all relevant authorities, a dilapidation report, fire service compliance and other regulatory approvals detailed in the six-page annexure.

This information suggests that, while there is no guarantee, the owners corporation at this time were open to receiving, discussing and, in this case, approving a major change in relation to common property, which makes us feel that a precedent has been set.

There is an additional by-law approving the penthouse level to extend the lift access to level nine, which again suggests the owners corporation is open to changes, particularly when they are indemnified from any expenses associated with the change.

## FURTHER RESEARCH

By searching the building street address online, you may find old listings in the building that have been for sale in the recent past. If they were listed through a real estate agent, you may be lucky enough to find the floor plans and some sales photos of these units. You may then be able to tell if they have been renovated and perhaps even if some walls have been changed.

In this building, records show that Unit 9 has been updated throughout in a plain but functional way, with no structural changes. However, Unit 18 has undergone structural changes where the kitchen wall has been removed and the kitchen has been opened up to the living room, which is exactly what buyers are looking for these days. It has also been renovated with a wow-factor look, a bold splashback and modern bathroom updates. This suggests that structural changes will also be possible for another unit in this strata scheme. There is no guarantee but there is a precedent and it's as positive a sign as you can hope for.

This suggests, also, that the kitchen/living room wall is not structural and with the right engineering plans you could do the same thing as Unit 18. You can also ask the selling agent for any details of renovations that they are aware of in the building and, of course, doorknock the owners of the renovated apartments and they might let you in to have a look at the work.

## THE VERDICT

This apartment ticks almost every box as an ideal unit to be converted into an apartment. In this case, the property was sold for $635,000 in a competitive market to an investor. While the unit sold above our $600,000 budget, the kitchen was in presentable condition, so there was some existing value in not having to replace the whole kitchen. It shows that investors are very savvy these days as to what they should be paying for the right type of unit.

The current owners of this unit are aware of the property's potential; however, to this point they have simply replaced the tired carpets with a quality floorboard and leased the property to tenants, with no changes to the existing kitchen and bathroom.

# PART III:
# RENOVATING TO SELL

# 19

# HOW TO ADD VALUE

Now that we have found a suitable unit, what can we do to add value to make it a viable flip? One of the advantages of renovating an apartment is that, unlike a house, there is a limited number of things that you can do to add value, and we can concentrate on the areas that will get maximum bang for our buck.

We can take our first cues from other apartment updates in the building. Simply viewing the before and after photos online provides a visual reference as to what adds wow factor. If you decide to hire a designer who is experienced in apartment renovations (see chapter 20), they will provide helpful advice in this area.

## STRUCTURAL CHANGES

Structural changes to the interior walls and doors will have the most dramatic effect on the floor plan's functionality. With the unit in our Neutral Bay case study in chapter 18, the two changes that make the most sense are:

1.  to remove the left hand kitchen wall, opening up the kitchen to the living room, the balcony and views

2.  to move the bathroom door to the hallway, so bathroom access is no longer directly through the bedroom.

By changing the position of the bathroom doorway, we will be able to have a sofa bed in the living room to act as a 'sometimes second bedroom' for a guest. That guest will then be able to access the bathroom without restriction, making it a very practical floor plan change that will add lifestyle value. We don't have the space to create a second bedroom, but we can create an easy sometimes second bedroom option.

Working with your designer, you can make a list of your preferred upgrades and costings. From this list, you can create a working document that will be the basis for your drawings and submissions to the owners corporation to meet their minor or major renovation requirements.

Let's set structural changes aside for the moment and look at the other renovation options that buyers will love. Take a moment to appreciate that most buyers will be looking to buy a finished apartment. Many will be simply an empty unit with new paint and carpet, perhaps some sheer curtains and not much else. Our goal is to create a sanctuary, where buyers feel safe, warm and happy to be home. They need to appreciate the differences between a unit and an apartment and how much work has gone into creating the apartment so that they are inspired to pay for the benefit you have created.

Let's start at the top.

## CEILINGS

Many 1970s buildings like 6–8 Hardie Street have what I call 'popcorn ceilings'. The actual name of this type of ceiling is 'vermiculite' – a sprayed and coloured concrete with a textured, popcorn-like finish. Vermiculite may or may not contain asbestos (see page 67 in chapter 9 for more about this) and was used extensively in the 1970s for its thermal and sound-deadening properties and its fire resistance. It was also ideal for concealing imperfections in concrete slabs. If you try to paint vermiculite with a brush it will absorb all the paint on your brush and you will dislodge it, making it look even worse.

There are two common options for tackling vermiculite. A specialist company can apply four coats of vermiculite recoat, which will leave you with a snowy white but still textured ceiling; however, you will still only have the option of track or hanging lighting. The other option, depending on your ceiling height, is to install a new 'shadowline' plaster board ceiling over batons. This will lower the overall height of your ceiling but will give you a flush, smooth finish with no edge cornices and the possibility of installing recessed LED lights instead of track lighting. The difference is the wow factor that buyers notice immediately, particularly if they are walking from a common hallway which has popcorn ceilings and into your apartment with a 'shadowline' ceiling. It's immediately a modern and aesthetically pleasing solution, which still retains the thermal and acoustic properties of the original vermiculite coating. If you have also installed recessed LED lights with dimmers, you are now competing with the presentation and feel of a brand-new apartment. Always use 'warm white' LED lights, as they make you feel you are at a home and it's what we are used to, rather than 'cool white' which have a brighter, slightly blue tinge and are more common in commercial situations.

In our case study building in Neutral Bay, if you search online for the address 9/6–8 Hardie Street, Neutral Bay, you will see the photos of the last sale of this updated unit in 2017 on realestate.com.au where the popcorn ceilings have been recoated and look acceptable for an update. However, if you then search for the address 18/6–8 Hardie Street, Neutral Bay, you will see that the ceilings in the photos from December 2016 for that unit have been plastered over and look clean and new. The light fittings they have used are still on surface rather than recessed, but they are a big improvement on the standard 'oyster' light fitting which is so common in these buildings and was retained in Unit 9 even after the updates.

## PAINTING

Every property will benefit from a good coat of paint. Many older units have not been painted for years and they look tired and uninviting, particularly if a past owner or tenant has been a smoker. In the 1970s, smoking was a popular indoor habit and left its mark on walls and ceilings of the day.

The secret to a great paint job is preparation, so be sure to scrape off any flaking paint from ceilings and walls and wash walls down with sugar soap before painting again.

If you do some research online and look at brand-new apartments offered for sale, none of them have a feature wall painted a bright colour, but many older units still have a feature wall legacy.

Colour trends come and go but a classic white colour provides a light and bright starting point, allowing the apartment to take its personality from the colour and texture of the furnishings. There are many popular shades of white. Some are warm white, which has a yellow/brown base giving a warmer hue; others are cool white, which has a blue/black base giving a crisper, contemporary feel. Talk to your designer about which white will work best for your property.

> ### Sold story
>
> I listed a unit to sell in which the living room had a single painted yellow feature wall and the bedroom a single red painted feature wall. The very first thing we did was have our painter paint the feature walls out and repaint the entire unit in a Dulux natural white. Consequently, the apartment was well received by buyers who appreciated its fresh look and feel.

## LIGHTING

Older units often have very basic lighting. In many cases, they have flat oyster lights, single hanging feature lights and a variety of track lighting everywhere else. This is an area where you can really make a difference. In addition to ceiling lighting, think about wall washing lights, floor lamps and table lamps, all of which allow you to create mood and interest without using overhead lighting at all.

## ELECTRICAL

If the power switches for your unit are located in a common area cupboard, you can add value by installing a switchboard inside your apartment. If a fuse trips, it's so much faster and safer to reset the switch in your own switchboard.

## Sold story

I sold an apartment that was ground floor and surrounded by foliage, so it felt dark. Although it had been recently renovated, the designer had used fewer light fittings than I would have liked. Although this gave the apartment a moody, modern edge, there was just not enough light. The first thing we did was replace all the low-level bulbs with the maximum-strength warm white bulbs available, which improved things, but the apartment was still a bit too moody. So we went to Ikea and bought three standing lamps that we could direct at the white walls and ceilings to increase the ambient light level with a wash of light. It was a simple fix that made all the difference.

## WINDOWS

Generally, the owners corporation own your windows and front door, so they can't be changed without authority. As windows are readily seen from the street, they are very much part of the look and fabric of the building, and consistency is important to the owners corporation. However, check your by-laws as sometimes windows and doors to balconies have been ruled to be the responsibility of the owner. Where a door and window combination open onto a balcony, you may be able to request changes from the owners corporation when they are in keeping with the building's theme.

## Sold story

I sold an apartment on the seventh floor of a tall building that had been renovated by an architect. He went to great lengths to have bifold doors to the balcony approved. The original silver aluminium single door and sliding window were aged and restricted the view and airflow. They also looked sad. There was no support in the building from other owners because no-one had asked to make such a change before, however with a full renovation of the unit planned, the bifold doors were integral to the emotional impact for buyers. After much debate, the owners corporation finally agreed, on the basis that the doors could not be seen from the street so they did not impact the building, but they had to be of the same silver aluminium finish.

The bifold doors were a huge success, and during the sales campaign many owners in the building came to inspect just the doors. Everyone loved them and wanted to do the same thing – for this change of heart, it took my client to go out on a limb and push for what he knew was the modern solution to the 1970s legacy. To be able to push back bifold doors across a four-metre opening added a new dimension to the living room. It literally brought the outside in and drew you to the otherwise smallish balcony to enjoy the panoramic view. It was the wow factor that contributed to the emotion from buyers, which saw the property sell for a record building price.

Often it takes just one owner with a vision to propose a change that will add substantially to the enjoyment of their property without affecting anyone else in the building... then more changes will follow. Many people do not like change but if you go about things the right way, you may just win them over.

## Sold story

I know of a strata building at 5 Milson Road, Cremorne Point, where the owners corporation voted to replace all the existing window/door combinations and balcony railings to comply with new regulations. Each unit was required to pay a special levy to fund the works. A one-bedroom unit was required to pay about $50,000 as the levy to replace the aged window and doors with new floor-to-ceiling sliding glass doors and new glass balconies.

The whole building needed to be scaffolded and the works took several months, but the results have been a huge success and the before and after pictures will impress. If you search online for the property address you should see images in the public domain of Unit 11 showing the original window/door and balcony railing off the living room.

Then compare these with the photos of 20/5 Milson Road, Cremorne Point, to see the difference the upgrade has made.

Apartments on busy roads or in noisy locations will benefit from treating the windows with some sort of system to reduce the noise. I have sold properties which had windows retrofitted with a double glazing system: in essence, they install another level of glazing made from acrylic inside the window, which is held in place by magnets to make it easy to install and manage. The system claims to reduce noise and improve thermal performance of your windows by up to 70 per cent at an affordable price without replacing your windows. From my experience, they do a pretty good job of reducing road noise. Have a look at the Magnetite website, www.magnetite.com.au.

## Sold story

I sold an apartment on busy Spit Road, Mosman, that faced the main road. The original windows had been replaced by full double-glazed European-style windows that featured tilt-and-swing open positions. This was one unit in a building of 12 that had requested and had approval for the replacement windows from the owners corporation. The cost was entirely at the owner's expense, however the effect was almost silence with the ability to still open the window easily at any time for fresh air or cleaning. The first thing buyers mention when they walk into an apartment with double glazing is that they can't believe it can be so quiet. Double glazing adds value and the property will appeal to a broader range of buyers, so it sells sooner and often for a higher price.

## BLINDS AND SHUTTERS

Windows need window furnishings, so don't forget about them. I purchased a one-bedroom investment unit off the plan in South Brisbane last year and as part of the purchase I could opt for the window furnishings package for an extra $3000. It was a no-brainer. Yes please, because if I don't take the curtains and blinds package, there will be nothing included at all. There's the problem, no-one gets around to putting in the blinds after purchase, so I am often asked to sell units with no blinds at all. It usually means a quick trip to Freedom Furniture to buy pre-packaged sheers and a fancy curtain rod. Some units that have been renovated have plantation-style shutters all the way through. They look great as a feature but are often not a total solution. Some shutters need to be closed so they don't get caught up with the doors when you slide them, and then they block the light. There may be better options, so talk to your designer.

It's an extreme example, but the best definition of 'luxe blinds' that comes to mind is in the 2006 movie *The Holiday*, where Kate Winslet's character swaps houses with Cameron Diaz's character and discovers that the Beverly Hills mansion master bedroom has remote-controlled blackout blinds. She screams with delight, as I am sure everyone else watching was thinking, 'I want blinds like that in my bedroom!'

---

### Sold story

Recently I sold a one-bedroom apartment which had no blinds, curtains or shutters. That's not uncommon but sometimes they serve the purpose of providing privacy, not just looking good. In this case, there was line of sight from the toilet if the bathroom door was left open, which probably happens from time to time, all the way across the bedroom, out the window, across the street to the living room/balcony of the neighbouring building. It got me wondering, so I tested it and unlike that sticker on the back of big trucks that reads, 'If you can't see my mirrors I can't see you', in this case I could see them plain as day and they waved back when I waved.

---

## FLOORS

Your older-style unit will most likely have carpet in the bed-room and living room, lino in the kitchen, tiles in the bathroom and concrete on the balcony. The variation may be some type of parquetry timber floor in the living room. These days, every second buyer talks about their allergies and how they can't live with carpet anymore. That's a big tick for a timber floor, and you have a choice of engineered boards or laminate depending on your budget, but both will be more buyer friendly than carpet in the living room. Talk to your designer about the pros and cons of each and remember your target market. I would spend the extra to have engineered boards, they look better and sound better as well.

I am not a fan of tiles on the floor in the kitchen because they are so unforgiving. Being a bit clumsy, if I drop something on a tile it's broken, but with any other more forgiving surface, it may have a small chance of survival. Bathrooms are a tile area and I prefer carpet in bedrooms. Some people don't like carpet in the bedroom so it will end up being your choice. If you do carpet, it won't be a big space so choose a quality wool carpet, not a synthetic type. Carpet people can tell the difference and the investment is worth it.

### Sold story

I was asked to sell a unit but it had a funny smell that just wasn't right. It turned out to be from the carpet, which although it looked okay wasn't particularly new or attractive, so I recommended that the owner lay new carpet for the sale. This isn't always my advice but, in this instance, the funny smell made the decision for me. The new carpet had a new carpet smell and buyers were happy to remove their shoes before coming in the front door because that was the right thing to do. The buyer loved to be able to walk barefoot across the carpet and that feeling helped get the sale over the line. My thoughts are that if a buyer wouldn't want to lay down on the carpet then they won't want to buy the apartment.

## BALCONY

The balcony floor is often ignored. In your unit it will either be plain concrete or tiled, hopefully using a plain tile. In some units I have seen artificial grass improve the look of a balcony, with little preparation and no issue with drainage; sometimes, however, it just doesn't look right. It's probably better than plain concrete. By the way, if you paint plain concrete it just looks like painted plain concrete so it can often draw more attention when painted than by leaving it alone.

If you have tiles and they have a pattern that dates them, you may be able to replace them or, depending on drainage and the doorway height, you may be able to tile over the existing tiles (or plain concrete). If you do go for tiles, make sure they are slip proof, because it will be a wet area at some time or another. The other option that is popular with tenants who want to upgrade their balcony without getting permission is to buy pre-made timber or timber-look squares that clip together and allow water to pass through the spaces so that there is no drainage issue. They may also be called 'wooden pavers', 'deck squares' or 'timber tiles'. They can easily be cut to size to fit and as they are not fastened down and they can't be seen from the street, there is no issue with the owners corporation. Have a look at the Northern Rivers Recycled Timber website to see some examples: www. northernriverstimber.com.au.

The other forgotten opportunity is when you have a red brick or blonde brick balcony facing the inside of your unit. Whenever you look out, the only things you see are the tired old bricks looking back at you – yes, you can pressure-wash them so they look clean, but they are owners corporation property even though you are the only owner to see them. I know of several unit owners who have had blue board cement sheeting cut and screwed to the inside of their balconies, giving a flat, smooth finish edge to edge with the bricks so it can't be seen from the street. This allows you to paint or render the blue board to match your interiors so that, looking out on the balcony, it seems more of an extension of the living room than a 1970s time warp. You may find that another owner in the building has already done the same thing. Obviously, you can't do it with a glass balcony, nor would you want to, but a smooth balcony wall and a dressed balcony floor come together to add visual value and a bit of 'luxe'.

## AIRFLOW

If you are double glazing for traffic noise reasons, then you also need to look at air conditioning; the two go hand in hand. In Europe, with its extremes of temperature, any good hotel suite will have double glazed windows and air conditioning. In some areas of Australia air conditioning is a given, but in Sydney, for instance, we pretend it doesn't really get that hot. However, if our goal is to 'luxe it up' then air conditioning is a must when we double glaze the windows. Every new apartment on the market will offer air conditioning, so to compete with them we need to include air conditioning in our upgrade as well. It's no longer considered a luxury, as reverse cycle air conditioning provides both heating and cooling, which makes it a lifestyle choice.

Ideally, we still have the option of not using air conditioning and opening the windows and doors for cross flow ventilation – in my mind, having the choice is luxury. One split-system air conditioner with the header unit well positioned will heat and cool your whole apartment. The condenser unit needs to be outside so, depending on your building, it will most likely have to sit on your balcony. Some owners corporations allow them to be wall mounted on the building itself; this may depend on where your unit is located in the building. If the condenser needs to sit on your balcony, you can hide it with a timber slat screen, so it is still able to 'breathe' but doesn't dominate the space.

There are two other opportunities to create airflow which are worth discussing. One is in the bathroom and the other is the range hood in the kitchen.

Most older units have a bathroom with an opening window, while most new apartments have no windows in the bathroom at all. I much prefer a window to allow fresh air in and bathroom steam out. Older apartments with tenants often have a history of mould and it's generally not the fault of the unit, it's usually because the bathroom window is constantly closed and there is no other form of ventilation. The solution is to open the window or, in some cases, also add an exhaust fan connected to the light switch circuit, so that if the light is switched on then the default is that the exhaust fan comes on as well. Some exhaust fans are designed to stay on for a few minutes even after the light has been switched off, to ensure the bathroom is cleared of steam and moisture. One way or another, adequate bathroom ventilation is a must.

The most overlooked item in a one-bedroom unit will be the ducting of the range hood fan over the cooktop in the kitchen. Most units have a small range hood with a built-in extractor fan and two downlights. The problem is, 99 per cent of them just circulate the extracted air inside the cupboard because they are not ducted to the outside of the building. It's a lot more work to do it and it will require owners corporation approval for an external vent on the building, but it is certainly worth the trouble – again, every new apartment will have a ducted fan so ours should too. I have seen some ducting run through cupboards, or on top of kitchen cupboards to the cavity brick wall, where the air is dispersed inside the wall without an external vent. That may be an option, depending on the owners corporation of course.

## DINING

You have to eat somewhere, but eating TV dinners on your lap went out with your 1970s flower-power wallpaper so hopefully you have room for a dining table and four chairs. A dedicated dining table and chairs is often seen as a luxury item in a one-bedroom unit because space is tight, however try to fit at least a round table and four chairs to create the impression of a larger space than you may have. At the very least, you may be able to design a kitchen bench with an overhang so that you can include two stools as a breakfast bar option.

## STUDY NOOK

All the up-market apartments now feature some sort of study nook, so if we can include this as well, it ticks an important box for many buyers. It can be as simple as a bench along a dead-end wall just wide enough to take a laptop and high enough to sit with a stool, which takes up less space than an office-style chair. There you have it – an instant study nook. If you can create anything more, that's a bonus.

## TV CABLING

Cabling is always a challenge. It never seems to come into the unit in the right place.

### Sold story

I just sold an updated apartment and it was done really well but they had forgotten about the NBN and Foxtel, so the cabling came out of the top of a built-in robe and was taped to the wall over the doorway and then down to the NBN and into the TV. The TV was on a swinging arm mount but there was nowhere for the boxes and power cables. Every time I did an open home, I had to dismantle it all and hide it in the cupboard.

> I sold another unit recently where the antenna cable came into the room near the front door and was taped to the skirting board all the way down the entrance, taped to the floor across the kitchen opening and around the corner to where they wanted to watch TV. This apartment has new timber floors so it wasn't like you could just hide it under the carpet edge. It may be a lot of work to get the antenna/Foxtel outlet where you really want it, but it's so important.

Nothing looks worse than cables taped to walls… well, some things might look worse, but you know what I mean.

## STORAGE

No-one has ever said, 'This place has too much storage'. Just bear that in mind when you are upscaling your unit – storage is luxury. I sold an apartment last year where the owner had included some cupboards at the entrance specifically for shoes. They preferred people not to wear shoes in their home, so all the shoes were stored at the front door inside a cupboard. It worked very well.

If you happen to buy the top floor apartment in a small building, you may be able to negotiate with the owners corporation for exclusive use of the ceiling space above your unit. If the roof has enough pitch you can install a pull-down ladder and put down basic flooring over the rafters to create a storage space for light but bulky items like suitcases. When it comes to storage, you need to think differently to find opportunities that others may miss.

One of my investment properties has an open car space and no storage cage. However, to give my apartment the edge over others in the same building, I was given permission to install an above-bonnet storage cage – an elevated and lockable storage unit on legs. It sits against the wall of the car space and still allows the car bonnet to pass below it so the car can still park in the space. My property leased quickly because the tenant said it came with 'all the bells and whistles'.

## BATHROOM AND LAUNDRY

Older-style bathrooms are likely to have a bath with a shower over it and a plastic shower curtain, a pedestal sink, old-looking loo with exposed plumbing and an opening shaving mirror with storage for next to nothing. It may even feature a mosaic-style floor and a pink, yellow or green colour theme.

You do have the option to call in the professionals and let them spray-paint the wall tiles and the bath in white. You still have the same floor and fittings and, unfortunately, as big an improvement as it may be, it's still the old bathroom in disguise. Depending on your budget, this may have to do.

In my mind, the bathroom and the kitchen are the two areas that you will need to do properly to impress. The bathroom may also be the only place where you can put an under-bench front loading washer/dryer because you need the existing water and drainage to make it work. If there is no room in the bathroom, the kitchen is the only other laundry choice. If you are not keen on that idea, then it's back to the bathroom for a full redesign and the bathtub probably has to go.

The bathtub is a luxury but the laundry is a necessity so a compromise may be necessary. It's better to have a generous shower with easy level access plus the concealed laundry under a bench with a designer basin or two on top, than a bath and no laundry. They are my thoughts, anyway. Talk it over with your designer to consider all options and start from scratch to get it right.

If you are lucky enough to have a separate laundry, make the most of it. Stack your washer and dryer and put in as much storage as possible, particularly for the ironing board and the stick vacuum cleaner. Include as many cupboards to conceal shelves as possible and the space will look even better.

---

### Sold story

I had two apartments in the same building for sale at the same time. One had modified the bathroom with an internal laundry space and the other hadn't, otherwise the two units were pretty much the same. There was a shared laundry on the ground floor. The unit with the internal laundry was the first to sell because the buyers all said, 'I don't want to share a laundry unless I have to'.

---

## KITCHEN

This is the big-ticket item that is worth the investment. There is a saying that 'kitchens sell houses' – well, let me tell you that kitchens also sell apartments. The hard part of upgrading the kitchen is sticking to your budget. You can easily go over budget on your choice of brand name appliances alone. Getting the kitchen right, in my opinion, is best left to a designer. In the same way that I sell property almost every day, your designer will have the experience and knowledge to create a kitchen you will be proud of that will deliver that wow factor, so I would leave it to the experts. (See chapter 20 for more information.)

That said, you are looking for great bench space, great storage, clean lines, clever design and a timeless feel. Kitchens can date a unit faster than any other room, so choose classic looks that will stand the test of time.

### Sold story

I sold an older-style unit with a very old kitchen and the thing that the buyer was most excited about in the whole unit was replacing the kitchen. I was the first person invited back to enjoy a glass of champagne in the new kitchen. Quite simply, kitchens create emotion.

We have included a value-add checklist on page 173.

## 20

# PLANNING AND PROJECT MANAGEMENT

So, you've chosen a terrific apartment to flip and picked out what you want to upgrade to achieve a premium price in six months or so. Above all else, your successful renovation starts with a high level of preparation. First, you need to put together two main documents: a scope of works and a budget.

## SCOPE OF WORKS

Your starting point is to detail exactly what works are to be done – this is your scope of works. Write it up as an exhaustive list, room by room, so that you can see at a glance what has to be done. This will give you an easy-to-follow plan which you can then cost to create a budget.

Unless you're very experienced with interior design and know exactly how to surprise and delight your target buyer, I recommend working with a designer who has a good track record of unit upgrades and who is familiar with working in the strata realm. As you already know, there are many rules and regulations to follow, which is what discourages some people and makes the opportunity for you more rewarding. The best way to find a designer is word of mouth: ask real estate agents in your area who they know who has a great track record. They will probably charge an initial consultation fee and then an hourly rate or retainer depending on the scope of works required.

## Style and inspiration

Whether you're using a designer or going DIY, it's useful to do some initial online research to ensure that you choose a cohesive overall look for your project that will resonate with buyers. Avoid mixing styles in the limited space of a unit: if you're going down the Scandinavian path, stick with that theme, or if you are doing dark woods and contrast, do it throughout.

So, where do you go for inspiration? There are several websites that enable you to put some thoughts together and create a picture board of rooms and styles that you like, so you will have a starting point when you talk with designers or project managers. Pinterest (www.pinterest.com.au) allows you to create boards where you can pin images you like, and also provides inspiration via boards collated by various designers.

You might also check Houzz Australia (www.houzz.com.au), which offers 18 million interior design images and decorating ideas. Property styling websites such as the following are another good source of ideas:

- Advantage Property Styling, www.advantagestyling.com.au

- Canvas Home Interiors, www.canvashomeinteriors.com

- Coco Republic Property Styling, www.cocorepublic.com.au/property-styling

- Furnish and Finish Property Styling, www.furnishandfinish. com.au

- Valiant, valiant.com.au/interiors/property-styling.

## YOUR BUDGET

The more detailed your scope of works, the easier it will be to create and stick to your budget. Don't forget to include any council fees, owners corporation bonds, designers' fees and, of course, a generous contingency. If you choose to use a designer, they will help you with all of this and will provide a reality check on what can be achieved with your budget.

As I said earlier, it's all about the numbers. Our example back in chapter 3 was a $600,000 purchase with a $50,000 renovation budget for a 10 per cent to 20 per cent upside, depending on how the market values your location and quality. Given your budget, can you give the property the luxe factor that will set it apart from other properties on the market?

## OWNER/BUILDER OR OUTSOURCE TO A SPECIALIST?

While *The Block* contestants appear to be your average Joes, many of them also have hidden talents from holding down day jobs as carpenters, electricians, project managers or designers. Your own skills and talents will be tested in your renovation challenge when you decide to renovate to flip.

For any renovation, there needs to be a project manager – someone to say yes and no and keep everything on track to meet your deadline. Are you going to wear the project manager's hat, and possibly other hats as well, or are you going to outsource the responsibility to a specialist?

Are you going to be the foreman, on the job with your own skills to help keep costs down and ensure the quality of the build, or are you going to subcontract that role as well?

Basically, you need to decide whether you're going to be the client of a contractor or the owner/builder of the renovation. It's an easy decision if you have a job and work for someone else – you simply won't have the time to DIY.

## WORKING WITH TRADIES

If you choose to take on the owner/builder role, you will be responsible for hiring your own trades, coordinating their time and checking on the quality of their work throughout the project. While this sounds simple enough, it will feel a little like herding cats at times, so be prepared for some challenges. I have a love/hate affair with tradies because it is so hard to find a consistently good tradie. The tradespeople you choose and use will determine the quality, timing and cost of your renovation.

Here are some things to look out for.

### Are they licensed?

Your tradies must be licensed for the property renovations you're contracting them to do, whether it's electrical work, plumbing, gasfitting or waterproofing. They may be required to supply a safety or compliance certificate on completion of the work, so ask to see their licence. If in doubt, you should check their builder contractor or tradesperson licence with the appropriate organisation in your state (see appendix B for details). There should be records of the type of work they are licensed to do, and of any issued public warnings or finalised disciplinary action against them.

### Are they insured?

Licensed tradies should also be insured to an appropriate dollar amount to suit the type of work they are doing. Ask to see that their insurance cover is up to date.

### Are they experienced?

Being licensed and qualified are two different things. You'd expect, for example, that an electrician would be experienced in all aspects of his or her trade; however, many know the theory but have had no experience doing it. I know an electrician who restricts his business to simple inside jobs like changing over existing switches and replacing light bulbs for strata work – he won't do anything more complicated than that.

Many tradespeople learn on the job at your expense and actually need supervision at all times, but they won't tell you that.

## Tradie story

We once had a plumber turn up to fix a shower while we were not present. He decided he needed to access the pipe from the ceiling below, so he cut a hole in the bathroom ceiling below. However, the pipe was not the problem so it was a wasted effort. Instead of making a call to us about the problem he had created, he charged us for the two-hour round trip he took to Bunnings to buy a plastic vent to fit in the hole he had made. It looked awful and there was no need for it. We actually had a plasterer working on site the following day, who then had the extra job of removing the vent and replastering the bathroom ceiling. The plumber was convinced he had solved the problem he had created by fitting a vent and that we would pay for his time and effort to fix it. As you can imagine, we didn't agree.

This is why trade references are golden – particularly from local people for whom the tradie has recently worked, verifying that they did what they agreed to do in a timely and professional manner.

## Who's going to do the work?

Sometimes the owner of the business comes to quote a job and, after explaining the job to them, you like them and hire them – only to find that it's their apprentice who turns up to do the job. This means you have to start over and explain the job requirements again, and the apprentice may be on the phone to the boss almost continuously. Even worse, the following day a different apprentice may turn up, and you may have to start over with the instructions because they didn't get a full brief from the boss. Often, you are paying an hourly rate for their time while they try to work out where the job's up to and who's done what.

Tradies also often subcontract jobs they don't have time to do. They call in a stand-by mate who isn't as busy as they are and pay him less than they quoted you, so they make a margin on his work.

### Tradie story

Our plumber once sent a mate to connect up a hand basin for us – and he connected the hot water to the cold water tap and the cold water to the hot water tap. It wasn't until we got home and turned on the taps that we realised they were connected back to front. The original plumber then wanted to charge us again to come and fix his mate's work.

You will probably find that every time a new tradie arrives on site, they will tell you the last tradie has done it wrong and will charge you to fix the other tradie's work, even though you have already paid the original tradie in good faith.

When tradies get really busy, you may even find that they will want to be paid upon arrival, before they even get started.

### Keeping an eye on the job

I have learned that tradies rarely say no to any job, no matter how busy they already are. They say yes and then try to juggle your job along with all the other jobs they have. This means they may turn up first thing, unload all their gear and spend an hour on your job, then leave half their gear and head off to another job without letting you know. If you aren't on site, you won't find out. We once had an electrician charge us for an eight-hour day, but our surveillance cameras showed him leaving the premises twice and only being on our job for three hours. If you're on site, I recommend that you keep a log of start and finish times to compare with the invoices you receive.

If you can't be on site, put in some movement-detecting surveillance cameras to keep an eye on things for you.

---

### Tradie story

We were expecting a kitchen benchtop delivery but were not able to be home at the time, so watched the delivery via the surveillance camera feed on a phone. We saw the two men carry the benchtop to the building and accidentally drop it on the stairs at the front door. It was clearly worse for wear and needed to be replaced, but they spent about three hours trying to make it look right. When that failed, the two installers told us that the factory had supplied the wrong piece and that they would have to come back next week. Their boss wasn't very happy to get our phone call, and different installers were sent to us the following week.

---

## Materials and supply trips

Tradies buy at the trade price. They often have accounts at their supplier and receive a steep discount off the recommended retail price – anywhere from 20 per cent to 80 per cent. There is profit to be had buying at the trade price and passing it on at retail.

I have found that even when I supply all the light switches and power points, one gets lost through careless practice. I know I bought the right number but the tradie is still short one item so they charge me by the hour every time they down tools to drive to the electrical or plumbing supply shop to pick up a missing piece – which isn't missing at all, they just couldn't find it. This isn't profiteering, it's just careless, but I have now paid for a switch or connector that I didn't need in the first place.

## Noise

In New South Wales, the Interim Construction Noise Guideline recommends that the use of power tools be restricted to the hours between 7 a.m. and 6 p.m. on weekdays and between 8 a.m. and 1 p.m. on Saturdays, with no work on Sundays and public holidays. Check with your local council about the guidelines in your state or territory. Most tradies start work at 7 a.m.; however, check whether your strata building has by-laws restricting the start time for noisemaking tools to 8 a.m. or even 9 a.m. You must advise strata management of your renovation plans in advance – especially in regard to demolition of bathrooms and kitchens – so that all residents are informed in advance about when to expect renovation noise.

Also, while the start time may be 7 a.m., many tradies travel long distances to a job and may arrive at the site early, depending on traffic. They rarely stay in their trucks or vans, preferring to get the job ready by bringing in equipment and setting themselves up, and while power tools are off limits before 7 a.m., talking loudly isn't. Tradies also love to have music playing on site, so often the radio is the first thing they turn on in the morning and the last thing they turn off at the end of the day.

## Keeping the neighbours happy

Workplace safety is the most important aspect of any job, and so it should be. Among other things, this means that tradies may have to turn off the power, gas or water. Not all units have individual connections, meaning that when a service is turned off it may affect others in the building. You will need to know this in advance and advise your neighbours accordingly in writing. Your strata manager will inform you of the notification requirements around disruption of service to neighbours.

As the owner of the unit, you must take responsibility for meeting these strata requirements and keeping your neighbours onside.

Tradies, on the other hand, breeze in and breeze out, and it can be a constant battle to keep the peace on a worksite when so many different trades are coming and going, and with all these people coming and going your neighbours may be getting fed up with you too! Parking is always an issue: everyone wants to be parked as close as possible to unload, but they don't want to move their car again so someone else can unload. Tradies will often park in the most convenient location for them, even if it's someone else's parking space.

## Rubbish

In my experience, tradies always turn up to site with a takeaway coffee in hand and wherever they finish that coffee, that's where the cup ends up. It could be in your unit, the hallway or a common area. I have never seen a tradie take a cup home with them.

They also take more tools out of their truck than they seem to need, and always seem to leave something behind. I have four new hammers, three extra tape measures and an assortment of hand tools that were left behind by tradies.

Another tradie habit is to put their rubbish in your bin – and always the wrong bin. In my council, we have a yellow bin for recycling glass and containers, but because it has the most space, it gets filled with every type of building material. It's almost a game: the tradies load my bins and I unload and sort their rubbish from my rubbish so that it will be collected.

## EMPLOYING A PROJECT MANAGER

A good tradie is worth their weight in gold, but they are hard to find, which is why I prefer to appoint a project manager to plan, design, hire and fire, keep an eye on things, be there on site to stop a problem before it starts and keep the peace with the neighbours. The buck has to stop with someone, and that someone has to be on site to deal with the expected and the unexpected.

### Tradie story

Recently I heard of an electrician hired by strata who was drilling a hole through a six-inch concrete floor slab in a strata building to run a TV cable – and he drilled into a water pipe buried in the concrete. Not only did it flood the apartment he was in, it also damaged the apartment below before they could turn off the water. Then a plumber had to come and make that drill hole into a football-sized hole so he could repair the water pipe. The cost of filling and setting the hole alone was over $3000, and had to be paid by strata. It was an unavoidable accident according to the electrician, who certainly had a bad day. The strata committee decided to have the building mapped for plumbing and wiring to avoid this happening in the future. The electrician was still paid and probably still dines out on the story. It's Murphy's Law at its best.

If you're a time-poor, enthusiastic amateur like me, you will generally be better off engaging the services of a project manager to keep the renovation on time and on budget. You'll need to find, interview and hire an experienced project manager.

I find that word of mouth is the best way to find a great project manager. If you're using a designer, you may find that they are also an experienced project manager. Talk to local real estate agents about who they have worked with in the past or if they have any clients they can suggest who are experienced in renovations and therefore worth talking with. Some builders will also be able to suggest a designer who they like to work with. If you can find the right team, you will save time and money on your project.

Your experienced project manager should impress you with their contacts; they should be able to draw on a full range of tradespeople with whom they have worked before. They will know the right labourers to strip and empty the unit. They will have the right tradies to prepare the space, including builders, electricians and plumbers, and will be available to ensure that they are following the brief. They will know what is on trend and where to source it for the right price. As mentioned earlier, in my experience tradies can double- and even triple-book themselves on smaller jobs and are very good at starting and not as good at scheduling the job to completion. Your project manager will help to ensure they deliver your project on time.

Not everything will go to plan, so you need a project manager who offers you solutions, and doesn't just tell you the problem. They will be able to source products at trade prices and know when to wait for an item or when to go with another if it is out of stock. They will likely save their own fee in the difference between trade and retail on your fit-out alone.

## Sold story

I sold an apartment which had been untouched for 53 years until the owner moved to a nursing home. He appointed a project manager to renovate his unit by updating the bathroom, replacing the kitchen, adding a built-in robe in the bedroom and giving the property a full paint job and new carpet throughout. The property presented as new and it sold above market in a short campaign to an owner who was happy to pay the premium to be able to move straight in with nothing to do.

# CASHING OUT

So, you've run the numbers, selected and purchased a terrific unit to flip, and have seen the renovation through its inevitable ups and downs to create a truly luxe apartment your target buyer will fall in love with. Well done! The last step in the process is to cash out and reap the rewards of all your effort.

This book is called *Flip for Cash* and was written to help you consider the options of buying a home unit to renovate and sell for cash. Of course we're selling for cash! What else is there, unless you are prepared to accept shells and beads or will trade your property for a second-hand Italian sports car? If you set out to flip a unit, then you need to sell and cash out to complete your goal.

While I won't go into great detail about how to sell your property (see my previous books *Sold Above Market* and *Journey to Sold* for that information on page 181), let's look at the crucial points.

## KNOWING WHEN TO FOLD

I have talked about a six-month turnaround as being a practical time frame in which to achieve a flip, and it is. Perhaps you are planning one flip, six months off. Perhaps you are planning two flips a year. Or perhaps you want to buy, renovate and hold. It's completely up to you, but whatever you decide to do, rest assured other people are doing this and when they do their homework and stick to their plan they are achieving great results.

### Sold story

I was asked to sell an apartment in McLeod Street, Mosman, NSW. The owner had purchased the studio unit at a heated auction and told me they had paid too much at the time: $675,000 in August 2016. The sales figures are available in the public domain. The apartment was an updated studio unit of 42 m² with no parking. It had an 8 m² balcony with close water views of Mosman Bay, although it was south facing so did not get any direct sun.

To see images you may like to search online for the property address: 8/6a McLeod Street, Mosman, NSW.

The plan when they purchased was to convert the studio unit to a one-bedroom unit by installing a plaster wall and sliding door to the bedroom area, which had a window, and re-marketing the apartment as a one-bedroom unit. The conversion and updates, including washing machine facilities in the bathroom, cost less than $10,000.

The owner spent about $710,000 including costs and their sale price expectation was $750,000. I listed the property on the market to auction in March 2018, with an original guide of $730,000–$780,000 and an adjusted guide during the campaign of $700,000–$770,000. On auction day, we had one bidder with an opening bid of $700,000 and a negotiated offer under auction conditions of $745,000. The owners dug in, saying they would not take less than $750,000, so the buyer walked away. The following day the owners called to say they would accept the $745,000, however the buyer was no longer interested. Had they accepted the offer, after selling costs they would have been about $15,000 ahead in a falling market.

The property was then listed with another agent with a guide of $700,000–$750,000 but did not sell so it was listed with a third agent and sold in December 2018 for $656,000 – a loss of about $75,000.

Ouch, but that's my point – to finish your project you need to cash out of it and take the money.

In the words of the great Kenny Rogers, 'You got to know when to hold 'em. Know when to fold 'em. Know when to walk away'. If the deal is 90 per cent right, then don't think of it as 10 per cent wrong, cash out and get on with your life or start the next project. I have always said I never sold the perfect property, but I have sold hundreds that were close enough.

## CHOOSING YOUR AGENT

You can't choose the agent you will buy your unit from, however you can choose the agent who you will sell with. I am a big believer in loyalty so may I suggest if you enjoyed dealing with the agent you purchased your unit from, and you are convinced they did an outstanding job communicating with everyone involved, and you feel like you probably paid a little bit much but you are still happy, then that agent did a great job selling to you and they will likely do a great job selling for you.

As well as that, if they sold you the original unit, they know and appreciate the time and work that has gone into the upgrade and they should be the best person to pass on that knowledge to a prospective buyer and make them feel excited about the opportunity.

If you feel like the agent you purchased from gave you the run-around and didn't impress you, then don't reward them with the sale of your finished apartment, as they may not deserve it.

You need an agent who understands that you won't be happy with anything less than a super-premium price, to maximise your profit for all the hard work and risk that you have put into this project. Be sure that your selling agent is going to work hard to deliver the result that will make you smile from ear to ear. For more information on choosing your agent, read my book *Sold Above Market*.

## PRESENTATION AND STYLING

We are selling the dream. Your unit is now an apartment. It's competing with the best of the best on the market and you want to give it the same opportunity to sell for a premium price as a brand-new apartment has. That means you must present the dream so there is no imagination needed. You need the help of a property stager or stylist, and their careful eye and on trend furnishings and accessories to make your space look and feel amazing.

Your agent will have existing relationships with local area styling companies, so discuss your options and go for the luxe look to create a breathtaking interior. It's incredibly important to choose the right size furniture, not too bulky, so that the apartment still feels spacious and offers 'generosity'.

The accessories will give you 'pops' of colour and lifestyle while upright lamps and table lamps will add the warmth and mood that will make buyers connect. We want buyers to short-list your apartment after inspection; they need to remember it as much for its feel as its look. We are creating an emotional buyer who will have the 'fear of missing out'.

> ### Sold story
>
> I was asked to sell an apartment and the tenants had just moved out, so it looked empty and sad. We called in the property stylist and a few days later it was styled to perfection. Each room had the latest trend in furnishings and accessories, which made the apartment feel like home. The apartment was sold in a week and the buyer asked me to put them in touch with the stylist as they wanted to buy everything in the apartment just as it was. They loved it all and didn't want to change a thing.

## INCLUSIONS FOR THE CONTRACT OF SALE

Your apartment is fully renovated and looking a million dollars. I don't expect to see any item listed in the exclusions in your contract of sale. Buyers will fall in love with your overall product and everything they see will help them decide to pay a premium price. When they fall in love with your choice of a hanging light fitting, it's not the time to tell them that it is not included in the sale. I would go one step further and add in some 'other inclusions' to help our buyers to connect. For instance, many units have a space for a refrigerator. Often it is a specific size to suit the cabinetry and it only looks right when the fridge that was purchased to fit the space is on display. Your buyer will know that they need the exact same fridge to recreate the exact same feel in this apartment, so don't make them beg, include the fridge in the sale price so they feel that you are being generous and understand their needs.

When your stylist stages the property for sale, everything they bring in will be excluded. Furnishings and accessories are not fixtures, or built-ins, and they are hired from the stylist, not owned by you.

The standard inclusions on the contract of sale that are relevant to an apartment are as follows:

- Blinds – yes, they should be included, they are part of the wow factor.

- Built-in wardrobes – yes, they are built-in, that's a given, so they stay.

- Curtains – yes, if you have installed them to suit the space, leave them there.

- Dishwasher – yes, it's built-in, it adds to the luxe factor, so it's included, no discussion.

- Fixed floor coverings – yes, timber boards, tiles and carpet are fixtures.

- Insect screens – if you have them then they stay, they won't fit any other space.

- Light fittings – if you install a wow factor light fitting, it must stay. Don't even think about taking it with you, it's an emotional part of the sale for the buyer.

- Range hood – it's built-in, so it stays.

- Stove – in this case they are referring to an upright stove, probably the type that you threw out when you updated the kitchen so it's a no-brainer, whatever you have replaced it with stays.

- Other – I'd include the fridge, to make your buyer happy. If you have built in a microwave with a trim kit, it must stay too. However, if the microwave sits on a benchtop, you can take it with you. (If you do have a microwave sitting on a benchtop then I'd get rid of it before you even show a buyer, it doesn't say 'luxe' to me.) Most new apartments include a clothes dryer, not the washer, just a stand-alone front-loader-style dryer. If you have gone to the trouble of building in your front-loader washer/dryer or combination of washer with dryer stacked on top, then don't take it with you. Leave it as an 'other' inclusion. The same goes for that flat-screen TV and the swivel mount on the wall – include them and your buyer will put a higher value on them in their mind than the actual value they cost you. Besides, the wall will need repairing if you take them away as you will have to make good anyway.

## MARKETING STRATEGY

When selling, your chosen agent will present you with their marketing strategy to ensure that your renovated apartment is seen by all the premium buyers looking for an apartment like yours. It's important to appreciate that when selling, we often rely on a four-week sales campaign to tell the world and secure our best buyer. When a sale doesn't happen in that four-week period, our timing may be out. You can blame the agent, you can blame the price, you can blame the marketing, you can blame the location or the presentation, but it may simply be the timing.

Sometimes, a little bit of patience and negotiation will help turn a buyer who is not quite ready to buy into a buyer who will pay a premium price for your property. The auction process will create the best offer on that day. If the price is lower than expectations, and can't be increased under auction conditions, often realigning your price and expectations with the market in mind to create competition will create a premium sale price in the following week or two.

Some buyers simply don't like auctions, so they wait to see what happens and when all the cards are on the table and the pressure of bidding on the day has passed, it's then a case of what will they pay to make the apartment their own.

## A MOSMAN CASE STUDY, SEPTEMBER 2019

Recently I was asked to sell a deceased estate unit which had not been lived in for many years. It was as 'original', as you could imagine, and was filled to the brim with stuff – some people would have considered it to be the home of a hoarder. The first job we had was to clear the property so we could see what sort of condition it really was in. We hired some manpower, sorted the good from the bad, donated the good and took the bad to the tip until, many loads later, the unit was in its raw state.

It was worse than we could have imagined. The kitchen was a shell, the bathroom was a wreck and the two bedrooms were just old and sad. With the contract of sale in my hand, I invited several owner/builders we had on the books to take a look and make an offer to buy it as it was. One buyer could see what the others couldn't, and his company purchased the unit for $781,000. He immediately began advising, notifying and negotiating with the strata manager and strata committee to renovate the unit within the bounds of the 93 pages of strata laws.

The buyer understood the importance of ensuring that every rule was adhered to and it took about 12 weeks to receive full approval for his design and renovation. He literally replaced everything on the inside of the unit, starting with the ceilings, except for the windows and exterior doors, which are strata property. The unit is on the third floor of a 56-year-old building with one lift and an open staircase but did include a single car space, which was invaluable for tradespeople and storage during the renovation.

The buyer had a vision of a modern apartment with luxury highlights to complement the desirable water view of Balmoral

Beach from the small balcony. The second bedroom was a bit on the small size, however the kitchen area was opened up to flow into the dining/living space. There was a full internal laundry, in which the owner was able to add a second guest toilet – it was back to back with the main bathroom so he was able to use the existing plumbing.

Using a combination of his own skills, his project management ability, hiring the right tradespeople, tiling the two wet areas right to the ceiling, creating extra storage space and working with a known cabinet supplier, he was able to create a relaxing and luxurious retreat with high-quality finishes and a wonderful ambience that had anyone who went inside feel like they were stepping into 'something special'.

The owner called me in on completion and said he had hoped to spend about $80,000 on the renovation but because of the age of the building (56 years), he'd spent closer to $100,000. The property acquisition costs with stamp duty were about $812,000 plus $100,000 on the renovation, making his investment total about $912,000.

You may like to see photos in the public domain by searching 34/2 Clifford Street, Mosman, NSW.

I listed the apartment with an auction guide price of $1,000,000–$1,100,000 and, over the course of three weeks, some 75 groups of buyers inspected the apartment. Every one of them thought the renovation was 'really well done'.

Three days prior to auction, the apartment sold to an owner-occupier who just loved the fact that the home was so beautifully finished, just the way she would have done it herself. The sale price was $1,100,000, with agent and marketing costs of about $25,000, meaning a pre-tax profit for my investor client of some $163,000 in an eight-month turnaround, not including the cost of his own time and effort.

## IS THE TIME RIGHT FOR FLIPPING?

At the time of writing, the Reserve Bank has just cut interest rates to an historical low of 0.75 per cent. The media is reporting the first overall small increase in Sydney property prices, signalling that an upward trend may be imminent and that prices are likely on the rebound. Regulators and banks are reportedly doing what they can to get credit flowing again, with plans to relax a key lending benchmark that will assist some buyers' ability to borrow.

Unemployment has fallen for the first time in three years. The Senate has just delivered a $158 billion income tax cut package and finance brokers are saying there has never been a better time to invest in property. Even retailers who painted a bleak picture before the 2019 federal election are almost upbeat with a positive outlook for spending, with one newspaper headlining, 'Retailers bask in a little ray of sunshine'. These are all indicators that we are heading towards interesting times in the property market, and with that comes opportunity.

Nothing is a given and there is risk involved in renovation, but it can also be a lot of fun to turn an ugly duckling unit into a pretty swan of an apartment. There is a great sense of achievement in creating something awesome and you may find that you have a real knack for adding value and that the finished apartment may even surprise you. I wish you every success on your property journey, flipping units into apartments, turning a profit and having some fun along the way.

# Appendix A

# TAXES, DUTIES AND LEGISLATION

Each state and territory in Australia has its own property-related legislation, land tax and stamp duty. The relevant websites containing this information are listed below. Note that capital gains tax (CGT) is a federal tax; visit the Australian Taxation Office website for more information: www.ato.gov.au/General/Capital-gains-tax/Your-home-and-other-real-estate.

### Australian Capital Territory

- Buying and selling property – www.revenue.act.gov.au/im-a-property-investor

- Strata title property (or 'unit title property') – www.planning.act.gov.au/build-buy-renovate/build-buy-or-renovate/buying-into-strata-living

- Land tax – www.revenue.act.gov.au/land-tax

- Stamp duty (known as 'conveyance duty') – www.revenue.act.gov.au/duties/conveyance-duty

**New South Wales**

- Buying and selling property – www.fairtrading.nsw.gov.au/ housing-and-property

- Strata title property – www.fairtrading.nsw.gov.au/ housing-and-property/strata-and-community-living/ strata-schemes

- Land tax – www.revenue.nsw.gov.au/ taxes-duties-levies-royalties/land-tax

- Stamp duty ('transfer duty') – www.revenue.nsw.gov.au/ taxes-duties-levies-royalties/transfer-duty

**Northern Territory**

- Buying and selling property – nt.gov.au/property/ buying-and-selling-a-home

- Strata title property ('units in a body corporate') – nt.gov.au/property/buying-and-selling-a-home/ways-to- buy-or-sell-a-home/buying-a-unit-in-a-body-corporate

- Stamp duty – nt.gov.au/employ/money-and-taxes/taxes,- royalties-and-grants/stamp-duty
  Note that the Northern Territory has no land tax.

**Queensland**

- Buying and selling property – www.qld.gov.au/law/ housing-and-neighbours/buying-and-selling-a-property

- Strata title property ('body corporate property') – www.qld. gov.au/law/housing-and-neighbours/body-corporate

- Land tax – www.qld.gov.au/environment/land/tax

- Stamp duty ('transfer duty') – www.qld.gov.au/housing/ buying-owning-home/advice-buying-home/transfer-duty

### South Australia

- Buying and selling property – www.sa.gov.au/topics/planning-and-property

- Strata title property – www.sa.gov.au/topics/planning-and-property/certificates-of-title/strata-titles

- Land tax – www.revenuesa.sa.gov.au/taxes-and-duties/land-tax/frequently-asked-questions

- Stamp duty – www.revenuesa.sa.gov.au/taxes-and-duties/stamp-duties/real-property-land

### Tasmania

- Buying and selling property – www.cbos.tas.gov.au/topics/housing/buying-selling-property

- Land tax – www.sro.tas.gov.au/land-tax

- Strata title property – dpipwe.tas.gov.au/land-tasmania/land-titles-office/strata-title-information-and-faqs

- Stamp duty (simply 'duty') – www.sro.tas.gov.au/property-transfer-duties

### Victoria

- Buying and selling property – www.consumer.vic.gov.au/housing/buying-and-selling-property

- Strata title property – www.consumer.vic.gov.au/housing/owners-corporations

- Land tax – www.sro.vic.gov.au/land-tax

- Stamp duty ('land transfer duty') – www.sro.vic.gov.au/land-transfer-duty

**Western Australia**

- Buying and selling property – www0.landgate.wa.gov.au/ for-individuals/property-ownership/survey-services

- Strata title property – www0.landgate.wa.gov.au/ business-and-government/Land-Transactions-toolkit/ strata-titles-policy-and-procedure-guides

- Land tax – www.wa.gov.au/organisation/ department-of-finance/land-tax

- Stamp duty ('transfer duty') – www.wa.gov.au/organisation/ department-of-finance/transfer-duty

# Appendix B

# TRADE LICENSING

Each state and territory licenses tradespeople in their own jurisdiction. Some useful websites for checking licences are listed below.

### Australian Capital Territory

- www.accesscanberra.act.gov.au/app/services/licence

### New South Wales

- www.fairtrading.nsw.gov.au/help-centre/online-tools/home-building-licence-check

### Northern Territory

- Builders – www.ntlis.nt.gov.au/building-practitioners

- Plumbers – plumberslicensing.nt.gov.au

- Electricians – electricallicensing.nt.gov.au

- Contractors – www.accreditation.com.au/Pages/BaseSite/ContractorSearch.aspx

## Queensland

- Builders and contractors – www.data.qld.gov.au/dataset/qbcc-licensed-contractors-register

- Electricians – www.worksafe.qld.gov.au/licensing-and-registrations/electrical-licences

## South Australia

- www.sa.gov.au/topics/planning-and-property/land-and-property-development/engaging-building-industry-professionals/practical-advice-for-selecting-a-builder-tradesperson-or-contractor

## Tasmania

- www.cbos.tas.gov.au/topics/licensing-and-registration/search-licensed-occupations/find-a-licensed-tradesperson

## Victoria

- www.consumer.vic.gov.au/housing/building-and-renovating/plan-and-manage-your-building-project/about-builders-tradespeople-and-other-building-practitioners

## Western Australia

- www.commerce.wa.gov.au/consumer-protection/consumer-protection-licence-and-registration-search

# VALUE-ADD CHECKLIST

Below is a handy checklist to refer to when you are considering the scope for renovations.

### Airflow
- Air conditioning is a must (because all new apartments will have it and you are competing with them). Consider installing a split system.
- Install an exhaust fan to the light switch in the bathroom.
- Install a ducted extractor fan in the range hood above your stove.

### Bathroom/laundry
- Can you take out the bath and redesign your bathroom to accommodate an under-bench front-loader washing machine?

### Ceilings
- Can you paint over vermiculite?
- Can you install a shadowline plaster board ceiling over vermiculite?

### Dining area

- Can you fit a round table and four chairs to create the impression of a larger space?
- Can you design a kitchen bench with an overhang so that you can include two stools as a breakfast bar option?

### Electrical

- Can you install a switchboard in your own apartment, rather than relying on a switchboard in a common area?

### Floors

- Is there carpet in the bedrooms?
- Are there timber (or timber-look) floors in the kitchen?
- Are there tiles in the bathroom and laundry?
- Are there plain tiles (or even fake grass) on the balcony floor?

### Kitchen

- Choose a classic look that will stand the test of time.
- Maximise bench space.
- Include as much storage as possible.

### Lighting

- Choose a mix of ceiling lighting, floor lamps and table lamps.
- Consider installing recessed LED lights instead of track lighting.

### Painting

- Paint over brightly coloured feature walls.
- Choose warm white or cool white paint throughout.

## Storage

- Is there plenty of storage space? You can never have too much!
- Can you convert loft space into storage if this is a top-floor apartment?
- Can you install an above-bonnet storage cage if the apartment has an allocated open car space?
- Can you make cupboards to conceal shelves?

## Study nook

- Can you add a bench along a dead-end wall just wide enough to take a laptop and high enough to sit with a stool (which takes up less space than an office-style chair), to create a study nook?

## Structural changes:

- Can you add a wall to make an extra room?
- Can you move doors to give better access the bathroom?

## TV cabling

- Is the antenna/Foxtel/NBN outlet in a useful place? It may be a lot of work to move it, but it's important.

## Windows

- Can you add bifold doors onto your balcony?
- If your property is situated on a main road or close to a railway line, can you retrofit double glazing to reduce noise? Double glazing will also help regulate the temperature of the apartment.

## Window furnishings

- Are there simple, attractive window furnishings? Any window furnishings are better than none – buy pre-packaged sheers and a fancy curtain rod as a budget option, or install shutters and blinds for a higher quality finish.

# GLOSSARY OF TERMS

**ACM.** Stands for asbestos containing materials. Identifies that the building includes materials with more than 1 per cent asbestos.

**Art Deco style.** Style of property built in the 1920s and 1930, characterised by decorative elements, horizontal geometric patterns and decorative panels at entrances, around windows and along roof edges.

**Borrowing capacity.** The amount a lender will lend you. If you already have short-term loans, credit-card debt or other property loans, your borrowing capacity will be reduced.

**By-law.** A regulation made by a corporation, local authority or a committee (such as an owners corporation).

**Capital gains tax (CGT).** Tax payable on the profits from the sale of investments. Most investors are eligible for the CGT discount, meaning they are taxed on 50 per cent of their capital gain at their marginal tax rate. (Consult your tax adviser regarding your individual tax position.)

**Capital works.** Usually refers to structural improvements to a property that will result in a higher value or an increase in (rental) income.

**Company title.** A form of ownership of property whereby a company owns the title (rather than an individual or a trust).

**Concrete spalling.** Also called 'concrete cancer', spalling is caused when water and sometimes salt enters a concrete slab and causes the steel reinforcing within the slab to rust and expand.

**Contract of sale.** Lists all the relevant information pertaining to the sale of a property, including names and addresses of the buyer and seller, conditions of the sale and inclusions. Once signed it is a legally binding document.

**Conveyancer.** A person or firm – often a lawyer or solicitor – that manages the legal process of transferring property from one owner to another.

**First Home Super Saver Scheme (FHSS).** Government scheme that allows a person to voluntarily contribute up to $30,000 to their superannuation and withdraw this amount (plus earnings, less tax) to buy their first home. Voluntary contributions include before-tax contributions, such as salary sacrifice, and after-tax contributions.

**Interest only loans.** Loans on which borrowers are required to make regular repayments on the interest component only; the loan principal is not repaid and remains outstanding. See also principal and interest loans.

**Lenders Mortgage Insurance (LMI).** Borrowers who borrow more than 80 per cent of the value of an asset will usually have to pay Lenders Mortgage Insurance. This additional cost can be thousands of dollars.

**Liquidity.** The time it takes and the ease with which you can buy and sell an asset.

**Loan to Value Ratio (LVR).** A ratio of the loan amount to the property's value, expressed as a percentage. For example, if the

LVR on an investment property is 80 per cent and the property is valued at \$400,000, the lender will advance \$320,000 and the borrower must fund \$80,000 of the investment.

**Low Deposit Premium (LDP).** A one-off, non-refundable, non-transferable bank fee that a lender may add to low deposit home loans. Designed to reflect the risk associated with low deposit loans, LDP is calculated based on the size of deposit and how much is being borrowed.

**Overcapitalise.** To spend more on improvements to a property than will be reflected in the increased value.

**P&O style.** A style of property built in the 1930s. Typically P&O style apartments have curved walls, some glass bricks and porthole-shaped windows. Named for the P&O shipping line.

**Principal and interest (P&I) loans.** Loans on which borrowers are required to make regular, predetermined repayments on the principal and interest components, so that the loan principal is fully repaid within a certain period (usually 30 years). See also interest only loans.

**Property manager.** Person employed by the real estate agent and/or landlord to manage an individual property for an owner. Their role includes managing tenants, negotiating the lease, collecting rent and conducting condition inspections.

**Security.** An asset (property) pledged to guarantee the repayment of a loan in compliance with an agreement. Security gives a lender legal right of access to the pledged asset and the right to take possession and title of it in case of default for a foreclosure sale.

**Sinking fund.** An amount of money set aside to pay for unexpected expenses or capital works that will be needed in future.

**Stamp duty.** A state-based duty levied on documents and transfer of ownership of homes and buildings. There are many stamp duty calculators online that allow you to calculate how much you will pay on your property purchase. It can amount to tens of thousands of dollars.

**Strata manager.** Also called an 'owners corporation manager' or a 'body corporate manager', the strata manager organises and runs the owners corporation meetings, manages the finances, keeps abreast of strata law, and is responsible for building maintenance, insurance and risk management and resolving disputes between owners.

**Strata report.** Provides all the relevant information you need to be able to assess the building, owners and finances to decide if the building is right for you.

**Strata title.** A form of ownership devised for multi-level apartment blocks and horizontal subdivisions with shared areas.

**Title.** The legal document recording a person's right to ownership of a property. There are various forms of title, with particular characteristics, e.g. Torrens title, Company title.

**Vermiculite.** A sprayed and coloured concrete with a textured, popcorn-like finish.

# ALSO BY GEOFF GRIST

For most people, their home is their biggest financial asset. Add to this the fact that moving house is the third most stressful thing that happens in life (behind the death of a loved one and going through a divorce) and you see why the decision to sell a property is not taken lightly.

67% of people selling their property said choosing an agent was the most stressful step in the selling process. You need someone who will support you throughout the process, do the very best job in the shortest period of time and sell 'above' market.

*Sold Above Market* gives potential vendors all the information they need to make the right choice and understand the whole process of selling property.

GEOFF GRIST

**JOURNEY TO SOLD**

*Your Passport to a Profitable Property Sale*

Selling property is a journey that can take surprising twists and turns – and there's a lot at stake! Your home may well be your biggest financial asset, so achieving a GREAT sale price, rather than a so-so price, can make a significant difference to your net worth.

As with any journey, planning and forethought are crucial to success. In this practical guide to your *Journey to Sold*, you'll profit from real estate agent and entrepreneur Geoff Grist's wealth of experience, gained over two decades in the real estate industry. He explains the entire sale process: from the crucial first step of choosing the right agent, to presenting your property for sale, negotiating offers and, finally, slapping a big 'SOLD' sticker on your signboard with a big smile on your face! *Journey to Sold* is your passport to a profitable property sale.

Available from www.majorstreet.com.au and all good bookstores.